BIRMINGHAM-BRISTOL

PORTRAIT OF A FAMOUS MIDLAND ROUTE

Part Two
Cheltenham to Bristol and Bath

STEPHEN MOURTON & BOB PIXTON

This pictorial work on the Birmingham-Bristol route has been published in two parts:
Part One covers Birmingham to Cheltenham, including the line through Worcester.
Part Two herewith covers Cheltenham to Bristol and Bath via Gloucester.
The whole comprises over three hundred photographs, mainly from the steam era,
forming a comprehensive record of this fascinating, vitally important and very busy part
of the British railway system.

RUNPAST PUBLISHING

Front cover:
Gloucester, 1963. When this magnificent portrait was taken, the steam era was winding down, but not yet finished, on the Birmingham-Bristol line. 'Jubilee' 45564 *New South Wales* roars away from Eastgate while a 'Peak' diesel traverses Tramway Crossing with a down express. And there is still plenty of steam on Horton Road shed, for workings on other routes around Gloucester.   *M Pope*

Back cover – top:
Cheltenham, 18 March, 1933. This picture was taken in the days when there were just two tracks from Cheltenham to Gloucester. Midland 3F 0-6-0 3258 is seen on a down goods at Cloddy Crossing.   *E R Morten*

Back cover – middle:
Mangotsfield, 1960s. 44663 takes a fitted freight through Mangotsfield having travelled down from Gloucester. The '0' mile post on the right relates to the section from here, Mangotsfield Station Junction, through the Bath line platforms, to Mangotsfield South Junction, a distance of 33 chains.   *G W Sharpe*

Back cover – bottom:
Bristol Temple Meads, 22 August 1929. Two 4-4-0s, a Class 2 409 and Class 3 712, receive attention from their crews. The Class 3s were top express power on the Birmingham-Bristol line during the pre-grouping era. In time-honoured Midland style, another loco would assist if the load was over the limit for the Class 3. *Author's collection*

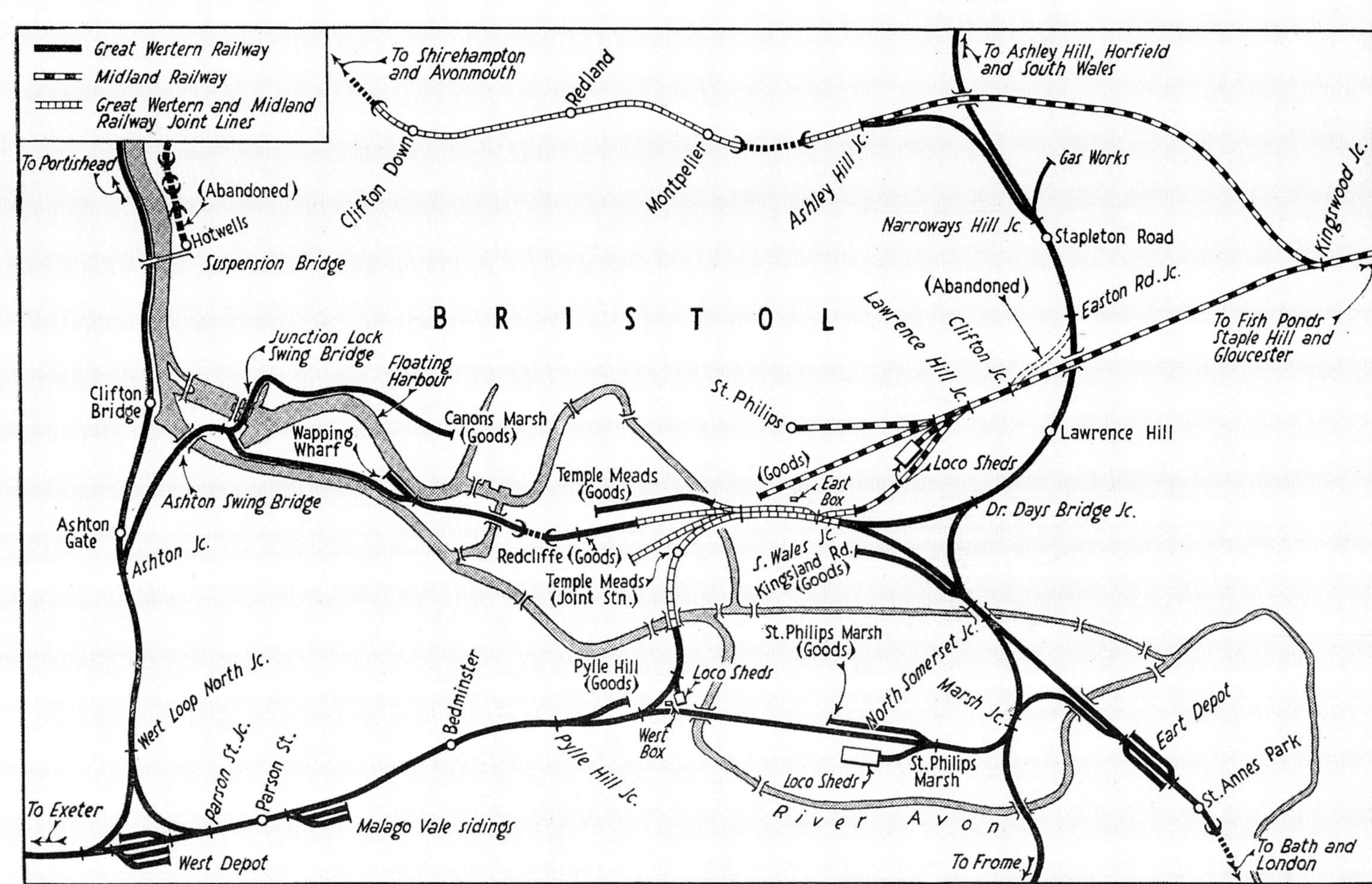

This pre-grouping era map shows the Bristol area and the Midland Railway encroaching into the heartland of the Great Western Railway. But it also highlights the fact that the two co-existed with joint lines in the area, including Temple Meads station.

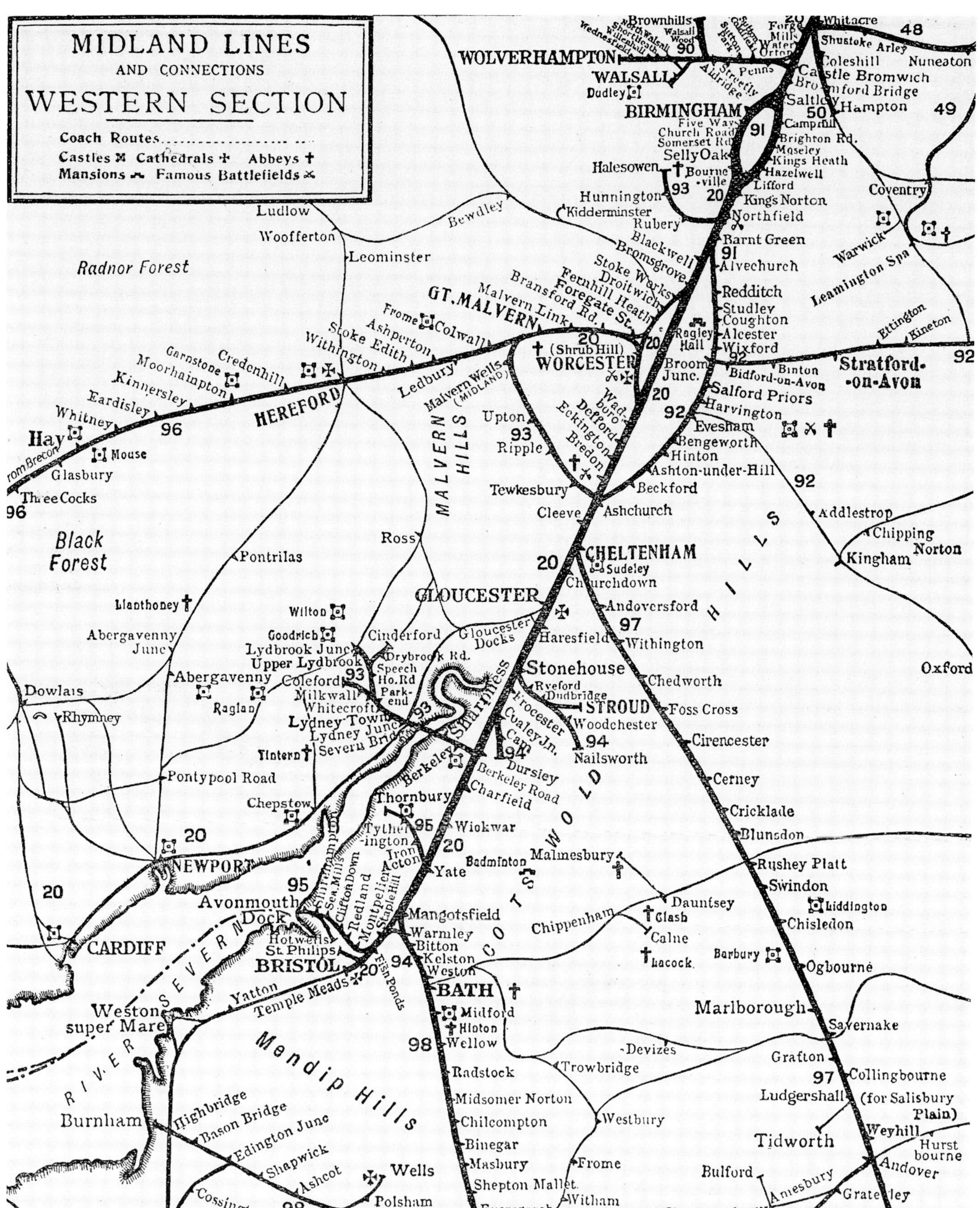

The Midland Railway provided this map delineating the Birmingham-Bristol route and connections in a 1919 timetable. It shows the Midland & South Western Junction Railway line from Cheltenham and the Somerset & Dorset Joint Railway from Bath, both of which were associated with the Midland, also the Midland route from Worcester to Swansea. But it deliberately ignores the competing GWR line from Birmingham to Bristol via Stratford-on-Avon and Cheltenham!

Cheltenham Lansdown, July 1906. Those were the days – a 'Spinner' and straw boater at Cheltenham. Part of the train, the 12.5pm from Bradford, has already left for Bristol, which is why the loco is halfway along the platform. This train splitting activity was more often done at Gloucester than Cheltenham. The first two carriages belong to the Somerset & Dorset Railway and it seems that on this particular working, they were attached here to go through to Bournemouth via Bath.

Rail Archive Stephenson

Introduction

This volume carries on the survey of the railway from Birmingham to Bristol and Bath, starting from Cheltenham station which has always generated a lot of passenger traffic – and, in the modern privatised railway era, enjoys a far better service on this route than its near neighbour, the city of Gloucester. Since closure of Gloucester Eastgate station in the 1970s, trains calling at the city on their way between Birmingham and Bristol have had to perform a reversal in the former GWR Central station, which takes extra time and has led to a high proportion of cross-country services cutting out the stop altogether by using the avoiding line. The route through Eastgate traversed several level crossings in the city, holding up traffic, very inconvenient in the car-mad age we live in nowadays. There were quite a number of wayside stations between Gloucester and Bristol Temple Meads, but they mostly closed in the 1960s, though some new stations have opened in recent years. Three branches left the main line in a six mile stretch – Stonehouse to Stroud and Nailsworth; Coaley Junction to Dursley; Berkeley Road to Sharpness and Lydney, all feeding traffic to and from the main line – only the latter is still partly open, as far as Sharpness. There were lots of holiday trains in the steam era bound not just for the resorts of the West of England, but also for Bournemouth via the Somerset & Dorset line from Bath. Add in plenty of freight trains, with big yards in the Bristol area at Westerleigh on the Midland and Stoke Gifford on the Great Western, and there were very few dull moments for the lineside observer. The old Midland route from Bristol up through Fishponds and Mangotsfield has also disappeared, along with the line to Bath, apart from a preserved section based at Bitton. There were loco depots for the route at Gloucester Barnwood, Bristol Barrow Road and Bath Green Park, with an ever-changing variety of motive power from many parts of BR. All of this fascinating railway route has hopefully been captured in this book and Volume One which covered the section from Birmingham to Cheltenham.

Stephen Mourton, Bob Pixton, August 2003

Contents

© 2003 Stephen Mourton and Bob Pixton

Published by Runpast Publishing, 10 Kingscote Grove, Cheltenham, Gloucestershire GL51 6JX

Typesetting and reproduction by Viners Wood Associates – 01452 812813
Printed in England by The Amadeus Press Ltd., Cleckheaton

ISBN 1 870754 58 1

The Making of the Route

The Midland Railway had an important connection at Cheltenham with the Midland & South Western Junction Railway which ran its first services into Lansdown in August 1891. This enabled passengers and goods from Birmingham and further afield to get to Southampton via the GWR line to Andoversford, thence Cirencester, Swindon, Marlborough and Andover on the MSWJ. Through carriages from the MR, LNWR and LSWR were very much a part of the scene at Cheltenham. The MSWJ had running powers from Lansdown Junction to High Street Goods station, and a small locomotive shed was constructed there, expanded to three roads in 1910 – a building still in existence at the time of writing. Improvements to accommodate the MSWJ at Cheltenham High Street and Lansdown were done by the Cheltenham Station Company, basically financed by the Midland Railway, so it was no surprise when the company was absorbed by the MR in 1895. The Midland Railway had running powers for all traffic over the MSWJ from Andoversford Junction to Red Posts Junction at Andover, around 59 miles, but not over the seven or so miles of GWR track from Lansdown Junction to Andoversford Junction and this prevented the Midland from using its powers. After the Grouping the MSWJ was taken over by the GWR in October 1923, who seemed to hold it in scant regard, reducing the Andoversford to Cirencester section from double to single track in 1928. The MSWJ was however a very valuable and busy route in the First and Second World Wars, with ambulance trains conveying wounded service personnel from Southampton Docks to hospitals in the Malverns as well as increased passenger and goods activity. In BR days troop specials still utilised the route to get to the Army camp at Ludgershall – 9 August 1953 saw three such trains up from Cheltenham including one of 14 coaches with doubleheaded GW Moguls. There were still a number of weekday passenger and goods trains between Cheltenham, Swindon Town, Andover and Southampton until November 1958 when Lansdown Junction was altered and it was no longer possible to run from High Street and Lansdown onto the Andoversford line, which became connected solely to the ex-GWR line to Malvern Road, St James and Honeybourne. Just one passenger train ran through from Andover then, terminating at St James, making it virtually a local service, at times which made it pretty useless for journeys over the northern section of the line from Cirencester to Cheltenham. The last regular service train over the MSWJ from Cheltenham to Southampton ran from St James in September 1961.

The section of line from Cheltenham to Gloucester was a bottleneck from early days until 1942, when wartime demands saw it enlarged from two to four tracks, the new tracks being largely on the east side. The line between the two places was open for traffic by the Birmingham & Gloucester Railway from 4 November 1840. The GWR started its train service from Gloucester to Lansdown Junction and on to Cheltenham St James on 23 October 1847. This was on the broad gauge and as the B&G – by now part of the Midland Railway – was standard gauge, the track was mixed gauge, leading to some very complicated pointwork at junctions. The GWR's broad gauge was converted to standard gauge in 1872. Various agreements between the B&G and the GWR's predecessor, the Cheltenham & Great Western Union Railway, had called for the line from Lansdown Junction to Tramway Junction, Gloucester to be built at equal expense and for the equal use of the companies. The section was the first joint railway in the UK, with the B&G maintaining the line from Lansdown Junction to a midway board at Churchdown, and the GWR looking after the section on to Tramway Junction. The GWR was also to maintain the signalling over the whole line. Churchdown station was a joint one.

Even four tracks were not always enough to cope with the sheer volume of summer Saturday holiday trains in the 1950s. Both up main and up relief lines could be 'on the block' between and even beyond Gloucester and Cheltenham. A lot of these holiday trains avoided Gloucester Eastgate station by using the South loop, a reminder of earlier times when GWR trains from Swindon to Cheltenham called at the 'T' station on the loop to drop off Gloucester coaches, which were tripped into the Bristol & Gloucester broad gauge station – which was adjacent to the Birmingham & Gloucester station.

The situation at Gloucester in the 1840s was horribly complicated and totally confusing for passengers. There is a well-known cartoon of the time depicting the chaos here caused by having two gauges, with passengers and goods trying to transfer between the two, and leading to questions in Parliament. The Bristol & Gloucester Railway and the Cheltenham & Great Western Union Railway used the same broad gauge station from the start of their respective services in July 1844. But in 1845 the Bristol & Gloucester, and the Birmingham & Gloucester, both became part of the Midland Railway, which was determined to convert the Bristol line to standard gauge. Meanwhile the C&GWU had become part of the GWR, still broad gauge, and, from September 1851, used the South Wales Railway station whose line from Chepstow was also broad gauge. All broad gauge lines around Gloucester were converted to standard gauge in May 1872, except the South loop which was taken up – and only reinstated in 1901.

Other developments so far as the Midland was concerned included the High Orchard line, standard gauge,

Templegate, Bristol. The frontage onto the Bath Road at Temple Meads is seen in June 1982. This was part of Brunel's Bristol terminus and included offices used by the Bristol Committee of the GWR. The united GWR Board also met here as did some GWR shareholders half-yearly meetings between 1841 and 1858. *Stephenson Locomotive Society*

to Gloucester Docks, in 1848; the Tuffley loop to the south on 29 May 1854, which was also when all MR traffic became standard gauge and was concentrated on the enlarged Birmingham & Gloucester station, with the Bristol & Gloucester one being closed and used for carriage sidings.

Midland trains still had to reverse in and out of the Birmingham & Gloucester terminus until a new, spacious, through station was opened nearby on the Tuffley loop in April 1896.

This station meant demolition of the MR loco roundhouse which had been here since 1851 and a new shed was built at Barnwood. In November 1898 the Midland opened the New Docks branch from Tuffley Junction to Hempsted, over the canal and connection with its other dock lines. The last part of the branch from Tuffley to be used was that to Gloucester Gasworks, to which rail traffic continued until 1970.

The railway layout at Gloucester has always been problematical. Even the Tuffley loop had a number of level crossings, increasingly inconvenient in the motor car age, so the loop and Eastgate station closed on and from 1 December 1975. Once again, trains on the

Birmingham-Bristol line had to use the 'other' station, the rebuilt ex-GWR one, and reverse. Operationally time-consuming in the modern post-BR privatised railway era, this has led to the majority of cross-country trains on the Birmingham-Bristol line avoiding Gloucester by using the South loop and the city is now poorly served by these services. Considering how many railway facilities Gloucester once boasted, it is now very skeletal indeed, with hardly any steam age buildings still in existence.

Moving on from Tuffley Junction where the MR and GWR lines out of Gloucester used to meet and run parallel, it is a short run to Quedgeley which was the site of a big military depot with its own rail system. There was a passenger platform here in the First World War with workers trains coming in from Gloucester, Cheltenham and Stroud. Munitions trains included ones from a large dump at Gossington in the Vale of Berkeley which was connected to the Midland by a branch between Coaley and Berkeley Road, closed by 1924. Rail traffic for the military ceased in 1976. Also located here at one time was a 'Dowmac' concrete sleeper plant.

Some very serious planning was done in the early 1960s for a large freight marshalling yard at

Brookthorpe, between Quedgeley and Haresfield, but the downtown in rail traffic meant it was not proceeded with – it seems likely to have been something of a 'white elephant' had it gone ahead.

Next came Haresfield station which was a purely Midland concern, there were no platforms for the GWR tracks. It did not exist in Bristol-Gloucester broad gauge days, opening on 29 May 1854 when standard gauge operations commenced. Like a lot of the small intermediate stations between Birmingham and Bristol, it closed on and from 4 January 1965.

Standish Junction opened on 8 July 1844, and was the junction for the Bristol and Swindon lines, both of course broad gauge at that time. Although the Midland was solely standard gauge from 1854, it was obliged to retain broad gauge track through to Bristol for use by the GWR. But the latter never exercised its running powers to do so and the broad gauge was removed over most of the route in 1872. Various other changes were wrought over the years, but alterations made in 1908, including a new signal box, survived pretty much until October 1964 when a new double junction was installed, providing for more flexible workings between the erstwhile Midland and GW lines.

Stonehouse came next and the branch for Dudbridge Junction, Stroud and Nailsworth left the main line here. Though goods traffic survived into the mid-1960s, long enough to be dieselised, the branch passenger service ceased in 1947. After the Grouping in 1923, some Lancashire & Yorkshire Railway 0-6-0s were used on the branches for a while. A coal concentration depot was located on the east side of the main line at Stonehouse in BR days, opening in 1967.

The small wayside station at Frocester seems to have led a fairly uneventful life from 1844 until its closure to both passenger and goods from 11 December 1961. There had been a short-lived branch to Frampton Ballast Pit for a few years from 1918.

At Coaley, called Dursley Junction on opening in 1856, was the branch to Dursley, around two and a half miles long. The Dursley & Midland Junction Railway was originally an independent concern; from May 1861 the Midland took over the loco used to work the line and from October 1861, the whole concern was vested in the Midland Railway. Though the branch passenger service finished in September 1962, freight for the Lister factory at Dursley continued until 1970.

Dursley & Berkeley station, opened on the main line in 1844, was altered to Berkeley Road in 1845. In 1875 the Midland's four-mile branch to Sharpness Docks commenced operations. While this was useful enough as a source of traffic, the branch took on greater significance from October 1879 when the Severn & Wye Railway & Canal Co opened its line from Sharpness over the Severn Bridge to Lydney and there connected with its Forest of Dean operations. The Severn & Wye had its own locomotives which worked through to Berkeley Road. In 1894, the Severn & Wye, the Severn Bridge line and the Midland branch to Berkeley Road became joint MR and GWR lines, though the Severn & Wye continued with its own management until the following year. Six Severn & Wye locos passed to the Midland and seven to the GWR. The latter company gained running rights over the branch from Sharpness Docks to Berkeley Road. In March 1908 the GWR opened the Berkeley Loop for goods trains, giving a direct connection from the Midland's Bristol main line at Berkeley South Junction to the Sharpness branch for trains from and to the west.

Charfield – for Wotton-under-Edge – will forever be known for the terrible accident which occurred there on 13 October 1928 (see page 15).

Wickwar station was another Brunel design, but on a narrow site. The up side had only a modest shelter. Just south of Wickwar station is the 1397 yards-long Wickwar Tunnel.

At Yate was the branch to Thornbury, opened in 1872. The branch lost its passenger service in June 1944, but remained open for freight, particularly stone traffic from quarries at Tytherington. A connection from Yate South to the GWR's Bristol and South Wales Direct (Badminton) line opened in March 1908. The *Locomotive* magazine of April 15 1908 commented:

'To relieve the congested state of traffic through the Severn Tunnel several goods and mineral trains are now diverted to run from Lydney (Otter's Pool Junction) over the Severn Bridge and via the Severn and Wye (GW and Midland Joint Line) to Berkeley Road, and thence via the Midland Line to Yate and Westerleigh Junction, joining the GW Badminton line near Chipping Sodbury. This implies using the GW running powers over the Bristol and Gloucester section of the Midland Railway.'

So far, so good but it caused all sorts of legal ructions when the GWR wanted to use the Yate connection for a new fast passenger service from Birmingham to Bristol via the North Warwickshire, Honeybourne, Cheltenham and Gloucester avoiding line. Having used the Midland line from Standish Junction, as it was entitled to do under old agreements, the GWR expresses would turn off at Yate South Junction and carry on over its own line into Temple Meads. But the Midland objected. This service would be direct competition for its Birmingham-Bristol trains. The MR claimed that the Yate connection was only to be used by the GWR to gain access for services going to the Severn & Wye Joint via the newly opened Berkeley South Loop. It wanted the GWR to use the Midland's own line via Mangotsfield into Bristol. Unsurprisingly this always seemed to lead to delays for GWR trains. The GWR went to court, won its case in November 1908, and started using its own route to Bristol from Yate South.

At Westerleigh was a mile-long branch to Coal Pit Heath, while adjacent to the main line were the main Midland sorting sidings for the Bristol area. The Coal Pit Heath line was open to goods by July 1832 from

Birmingham to Bristol distances – from 1960/61 working time tables		
Station	**a**	**b**
Birmingham New Street		0.00
Selly Oak	3.27	3.27
Bournville	1.07	4.34
King's Norton	1.12	5.46
Northfield	1.27	6.73
Barnt Green	3.50	10.43
Blackwell	1.35	11.78
Bromsgrove	1.27	13.25
Stoke Works Jn	2.10	15.35
Abbots Wood Jn	11.20	26.55
Wadborough	1.18	27.73
Defford	3.42	31.35
Eckington	1.06	32 41
Bredon	2.59	35.20
Ashchurch	2.11	37.31
Cheltenham Lansdown	7.17	44.48
Churchdown	3.13	47.61
Gloucester Eastgate	3.23	51.04
Haresfield	5.47	56.51
Stonehouse Bristol Road	3.00	59.51
Frocester	1.61	61.32
Coaley	2.07	63.39
Berkeley Road	2.33	65.72
Charfield	5.16	71.08
Wickwar	1.73	73.01
Yate	4.57	77.58
Mangotsfield	5.20	82.78
Staple Hill	1.29	84.27
Fishponds	0.54	85.01
Bristol Temple Meads	3.04	88.05
Mangotsfield-Bath		
Mangotsfield		82.78
Warmley	1.18	84.16
Oldland Common	1.25	85.41
Bitton	1.00	86.41
Bath Green Park	6.26	92.67

a: Distance in miles and chains from previous station

b: Cumulative distance from Birmingham New Street

Washwood Heath to King's Norton via Camp Hill –
7 miles 2 chains

Stoke Works Jn to Abbots Wood Jn via Worcester –
13 miles 70 chains

Engine Shed Jn to Tuffley Jn via Gloucester Eastgate –
2 miles 38 chains

Engine Shed Jn to Tuffley Jn via Gloucester avoiding line –
1 mile 78 chains

Yate to Temple Meads via Stoke Gifford –
12 miles 4 chains

Westerleigh Sidings –
2 miles 54 chains from Yate

Mangotsfield for use by the Bristol & Gloucestershire Railway – a horse-drawn tramway predecessor of the Bristol & Gloucester Railway and eventually absorbed by the latter – and another concern, the Avon & Gloucestershire Railway, which ran up from Avon Wharf on the River Avon opposite Keynsham. It was however August 1835 before the Bristol & Gloucestershire Railway worked through from Bristol St Philips; the route included an inclined plane at 1 in 55 up to Fishponds and a 514 yards-long tunnel at Staple Hill. It is noted in 'Midland Chronology' that the Coal Pit Heath branch was worked by locomotive power by June 1847. The branch was worked thus for about a century, becoming a siding in 1955. The sidings on the up and down sides at Westerleigh were added to and extended in the Second World War. There were four signal boxes here: North

Above: **Bath Green Park station.** The imposing frontage of the terminus at Green Park was fitting for a place with the grand architecture of Bath Spa. Though the railway has gone, the building remains and has been incorporated into a supermarket – from trains to trollies.
Stations UK

Junction, open from 4.40am Mondays to 5.50am Sundays, also 10.30am to 12.40pm Sundays; South Junction open continuously; East Junction open as required; West Junction open continuously. A steady flow of light engines for trains starting and terminating here, sometimes with brake vans, came from and to Barrow Road shed and St Philips night and day; some being used for staff transfers.

Westerleigh South Junction signal box was originally called Parkfield Colliery Sidings signal box. Parkfield Colliery had a claim to fame, being the last place on the Bristol-Gloucester line served by the broad gauge coal trains of the Bristol & Exeter (latterly GWR), until January 1882.

Mangotsfield had a station from around 1845. When the Bristol & Gloucester Railway opened in July 1844, the section from Mangotsfield to Westerleigh was mixed broad and standard gauge, the latter being for the Avon & Gloucestershire to gain access to Coal Pit Heath. It was the first mixed gauge in the country. A new station was built half a mile south when the Bath line opened in August 1869. It became famous for having platforms on two sides of the triangle of lines here.

From Mangotsfield to Bath was approximately 10 miles and the line became an important factor in traffic flows on the route from Birmingham, especially after the

Somerset & Dorset Railway opened its 63 miles-long line from Bath to Broadstone Junction, where connection to the London & South Western Railway gave access to Bournemouth. Many trains came down with holidaymakers from the north and curved off at Mangotsfield for a trip over the S&D and the resorts of Bournemouth and elsewhere on that coast. There was also some very useful freight traffic generated on the S&D, not least perishables.

Right: 'Table 28' shows the Birmingham-Bristol express train service as it appeared in the last published public timetables for both the LMS and GWR, effective from October 6 1947. The one printed here is from the LMS table and shows that it had the vast majority of services. The 7am from New Street is rather privileged to be designated as an express, taking over three and a half hours. Hopefully no passengers made the mistake of going to Snow Hill on a Sunday to catch a Bristol train – there were none. The only basic difference in the GWR version was that Snow Hill station came above New Street and likewise Malvern Road took precedence over Lansdown! It was not until 29 July 1951 that Gloucester GW became Central and Gloucester LMS had Eastgate added to its name.

Table 28

THROUGH EXPRESS TRAINS
BIRMINGHAM (New Street and Snow Hill) AND CHELTENHAM SPA, GLOUCESTER AND BRISTOL (Temple Meads)

WEEK DAYS

	a.m.	a.m.	a.m.	a.m.	a.m.	a.m. R	a.m. R
Birmingham (New Street)...dep.	2 0	2 40	7 0	…	9 30	…	1135
" (Snow Hill)..... "	…	…	…	9 10	…	11 10	…
Cheltenham Spa (Lansdown) arr.	3 1	4 1	9 19	…	10 31	…	1235
" (Malvern Road) "	…	…	…	1018	…	12 20	…
Gloucester (G.W.) "	…	…	…	1032	…	12†49	…
" (L.M.S.) "	3 20	4 19	9 37	…	10 46	…	1251
Bristol (Temple Meads) "	4 35	5 26	10 39	…	11 52	1 35	1 50

WEEK DAYS—Continued

	p.m.	p.m. S	p.m. R	p.m.	p.m. R	p.m.	p.m.
Birmingham (New Street)...dep.	1242	1 30	1 44	…	6 8	7 35	9 18
" (Snow Hill)..... "	…	…	…	3 45	…	…	…
Cheltenham Spa (Lansdown) arr.	1 39	2 27	2 59	…	7 5	9 29	10 59
" (Malvern Road) "	…	…	…	4 52	…	…	…
Gloucester (G.W.) "	…	…	…	5 7	…	…	…
" (L.M.S.) "	1 54	2 43	3 14	…	7 20	9 45	11 15
Bristol (Temple Meads) "	…	3 45	4 10	…	8 17	…	12 15

SUNDAYS

	a.m.	a.m.	a.m.	p.m.	p.m.	p.m.	p.m.	p.m.
Birmingham (New Street)...dep.	2 50	8 50	10 40	4 20	5 46	8 27	9 5	9 30
" (Snow Hill)..... "	…	…	…	…	…	…	…	…
Cheltenham Spa (Lansdown) arr.	4 19	10 50	11 42	5 22	7 37	9 28	10 20	11 4
" (Malvern Road) "	…	…	…	…	…	…	…	…
Gloucester (G.W.) "	…	…	…	…	…	…	…	…
" (L.M.S.) "	4 39	11 9	11 59	5 38	7 50	9 45	10 44	11 20
Bristol (Temple Meads) "	5 50	…	1 0	6 45	9 13	1045	…	12 20

WEEK DAYS

	a.m.	a.m. R	a.m.	a.m. R	p.m.	p.m.	p.m.	p.m. R	p.m. R
Bristol (Temple Meads).......dep.	1 10	7 40	…	10 20	…	12 35	…	2 15	4 45
Gloucester (L.M.S.) "	2 12	8 40	…	11 19	1258	1 26	1 40	3 7	…
" (G.W.) "	…	…	10 0	…	…	…	…	…	5†25
Cheltenham Spa (Malv'n Rd.) "	…	…	10 13	…	…	…	…	…	5 55
" (Lansdown) "	2 33	8 57	…	11 36	1 15	1 43	1 58	3 23	…
Birmingham (Snow Hill) ....arr.	…	…	11 25	…	…	…	…	…	7 11
" (New Street)... "	4 2	10 3	…	12 36	2 15	2 43	3 45	4 23	…

WEEK DAYS—Continued / SUNDAYS

	p.m. R	p.m.	p.m.	p.m. H	a.m.	a.m.	p.m.	p.m.	p.m.	p.m.
Bristol (Temple Meads).......dep.	5 0	…	7 20	7 35	1 10	8 10	2 0	4 40	7 20	7 35
Gloucester (L.M.S.) "	5 55	…	8 27	8 36	2 18	9 22	2 56	5 35	8 27	8 36
" (G.W.) "	…	6 30	…	…	…	…	…	…	…	…
Cheltenham Spa (Malv'n Rd.) "	…	6 47	…	…	…	…	…	…	…	…
" (Lansdown) "	6 12	…	8 46	8 54	2 39	9 40	3 14	5 54	8 46	8 54
Birmingham (Snow Hill) ....arr.	…	8 11	…	…	…	…	…	…	…	…
" (New Street)... "	7 12	…	9 51	9 59	3 53	11 22	4 19	6 59	9 51	9 59

H Fridays only.

R Restaurant Car
S Saturdays only

† Change at Cheltenham Spa (Malvern Road)

Principal year-round weekday through passenger trains on the Birmingham-Bristol line in late 1950s.

Down trains – expresses

M215	6.12am	Derby-Bristol
M229	7.35am	Nottingham-Bristol
M239	7.32am	Bradford-Bristol
1O95	10.15am	Manchester-Bournemouth
M287	8.15am	Newcastle-Cardiff
M251	10.15am	Bradford-Paignton
M295	12.48pm	York-Bristol
M307	12.43pm	Newcastle-Bristol
M269	4.45pm	Bradford-Bristol
M277	9.2pm	Bradford-Bristol
M321	7.5pm	Newcastle-Bristol

Down trains – locals

	7.0am	Birmingham-Bristol
	5.47pm	Birmingham-Bristol

Down trains – parcels

P489	9.23pm	Sutton Park-Bristol
P477	12.37am	Leicester-Bath
P481	2.0am	Derby-Bristol
P487	1.32pm	Derby-Bristol

Up trains – expresses

M204	1.10am	Bristol-Sheffield
M214	7.40am	Bristol-Bradford
M304	8.40am	Bristol-Sheffield
M308	8.30am	Cardiff-Newcastle
M310	10.30am	Bristol-Newcastle
M236	9.45am	Bournemouth-Manchester
M240	9.15am	Paignton-Bradford
M320	2.15pm	Bristol-York
M322	5.0pm	Bristol-York
M324	7.25pm	Bristol-Newcastle

Up trains – locals

	9.15am	Bristol-Gloucester-Birmingham
	6.30pm	Bristol-Birmingham

Up trains – parcels

P478	2.34am	Gloucester-Sheffield
P482	8.15pm	Bristol-Leeds
P484	8.25pm	Templecombe-Derby
P486	11.45pm	Bristol-Derby

UP LMR EXPRESS PASSENGER TRAINS SATURDAY 7 AUGUST 1954 at GLOUCESTER 8am-8pm

Train No.	Loco	Train		Depart	Load
302	44813	8.18	Gloucester-Leeds	8.20	7
216	45682	7.35	Bristol-Bradford	8.47	11
306	45264	8.30	Bristol-Newcastle	9.31	11
218	40407	9.50	Gloucester-Nottingham	9.50	8
835	44962	6.40	Paignton-Bradford	10.19	9
308	45620	8.30	Cardiff-Newcastle	10.39 C	10
220	44746	9.15	Weston-Super-Mare-Newcastle	11.09 A	10
995	44918	7.10	Paignton-Kidsgrove	11.18 A	13
222	45656	6.55	Paignton-Bradford	11.28	12
224	44919	8.00	Bournemouth-Sheffield	11.33 A	9
310	45572	10.20	Bristol-Newcastle	11.42	11
226	44745	9.52	Weston-Super-Mare-Birmingham	11.51	11
214	44741	8.16	Bournemouth-Manchester	12/04	10
314	44757	7.45	Paignton-Newcastle	12/18	11
228	44853	8.40	Bournemouth-Bradford	12/30	10
230	73004	8.40	Paignton-Nottingham	12/44 A	10
234	42767	9.25	Bournemouth-Manchester	1/04	12
232	42703	8.52	Paignton-Leeds	1/15	10
236	45449	9.45	Bournemouth-Manchester	1/23	12
240	45561	8.45	Kingswear-Bradford	1/39	12
834	44263	10.35	Exeter-Bradford	1/46 A	11
844	44534	12.30	Bristol-Sheffield	1/54	10
238	44826	9.55	Bournemouth-Leeds	2/05	11
994	44048	8.30	Paignton-Bradford	2/15 A	11
242	44986	12.45	Bristol-Sheffield	2/23	11
244	44666	12.15	Weston-Super-Mare-Sheffield	2/33	11
246	44815	10.08	Bournemouth-Cleethorpes	2/42	12
248	45662	10.15	Teignmouth-Bradford	2/47 A	13
250	44165	10.35	Bournemouth-Manchester	2/50	11
254	41117	11.12	Bournemouth-Derby	3/29	8
320	44814	2.15	Bristol-York	3/38	10
318	45654	8.10	Newquay-Newcastle	3/43 A	12
256	44851	11.40	Bournemouth-Sheffield	3/48	11
258	44424	2.40	Bristol-Nottingham	3/56	10
986	44697	12.00	Bournemouth-Tunstall	4/02 A	10
260	44663	10.58	Paignton-Nottingham	4/47	10
828	73051	12.25	Bournemouth-Loughborough	4/57	10
266	44747	3.50	Bristol-Bradford	5/06	12
268	43924	4.45	Bristol-Derby	5/52	9
324	45585	11.00	Newquay-York	7/06	14
270	45407	2.25	Paignton-Derby	7/15	10
272	45577	10.45	Penzance-Sheffield	7/58	12

- Trains marked **A** in the departure column used the avoiding line; **C** Central station; others Eastgate station
- Departure times of some avoiding line trains are approximate
- Furthest behind schedule was train 994, 126 minutes late
- Train 254 arrived with 44035, replaced by 41117
- In addition to the above LMR trains, 11 Western Region expresses used parts of the line between Bristol and Cheltenham during the period.

DOWN LMR EXPRESS PASSENGER TRAINS SAT 7 AUGUST 1954 at GLOUCESTER 8am-8pm

Train No.	Loco	Train		Depart	Load
205	44666	6 50	Birmingham-Weston-Super-Mare	8.35	11
209	44964	6.35	Walsall-Kingswear	9.00	11
213	44165	7.43	Birmingham-Bournemouth	9.24	8
221	44663	6.40	Leicester-Paignton	9.53	10
219	44814	2.55	Leeds-Bristol	10.04	11
223	44747	8.00	Derby-Bristol	10.43	10
225	44463	9.18	Birmingham-Bournemouth	10.52	8
227	42769	7.35	Nottingham-Bournemouth	11.01	11
229	45585	7.43	Nottingham-Plymouth	11.13	12
233	73011	8.06	Sheffield-Kingswear	12/42	11
237	45407	9.17	Sheffield-Bristol	12/43	10
988	42900	10.00	Leicester-Bournemouth	12/57	8
239	45577	7.30	Bradford-Bristol	1/02	12
243	73016	9.40	Sheffield-Bournemouth	1/16	9
241	44248	6.57	Cleethorpes-Bournemouth	1/36	10
245	45239	7.50	Bradford-Bournemouth	1/44	11
901	44743	7.40	Darlington-Paignton	1/59	6
283	45663	7.30	Newcastle-Paignton	2/38	11
W220	44775	10.25	Manchester-Bournemouth	2/47	12
249	45562	9.30	Leeds-Paignton	2/56	12
W242	73051	10.30	Liverpool-Bournemouth	3/15	12
649	73053	11.00	Sheffield-Gloucester	3/15	9
W196	44776	10.38	Manchester-Bournemouth	3/32	10
285	73047	7.42	Sunderland-Bristol	3/41	10
251	45589	9.25	Bradford-Paignton	4/16	12
287	45651	8.12	Newcastle-Cardiff	5/29	13
261	45275	12/37	Leeds-Bristol	5/56	10

- All trains went through Eastgate station, except 287 which used Central
- Arrival times are shown for trains 649 and 287
- Furthest behind schedule was train 287, 159 minutes late
- A further dozen or so expresses went through Friday night/Saturday morning before 8am, including four for Bournemouth

The Railway Correspondence & Travel Society did a London Midland Region Midland Division traffic survey on a peak holiday Saturday, 7 August 1954, basically covering class 'A' passenger trains. No less than 42 went up through Gloucester between 8am and 8pm – and those were just the ones bound for the north via the LMR, there were other, purely Western Region, holiday trains as well. On the down, a dozen or so trains ran overnight Friday/Saturday and, to add to the line's capacity problems, there were no less than nine pigeon specials. Several points are revealed by the 'up' table: twelve trains leaving Bournemouth between 8am and 12.25pm, all using the Somerset & Dorset line on their way to Gloucester and beyond; 7 trains departing Paignton from 6.40am to 8.52am; nineteen trains threading their way through Gloucester between 1pm and 4pm – also a busy period for WR trains; the liberal use of '4F' 0-6-0s. The intensity of summer Saturday workings continued until the end of summer 1962, after which through trains were diverted away from the S&D.

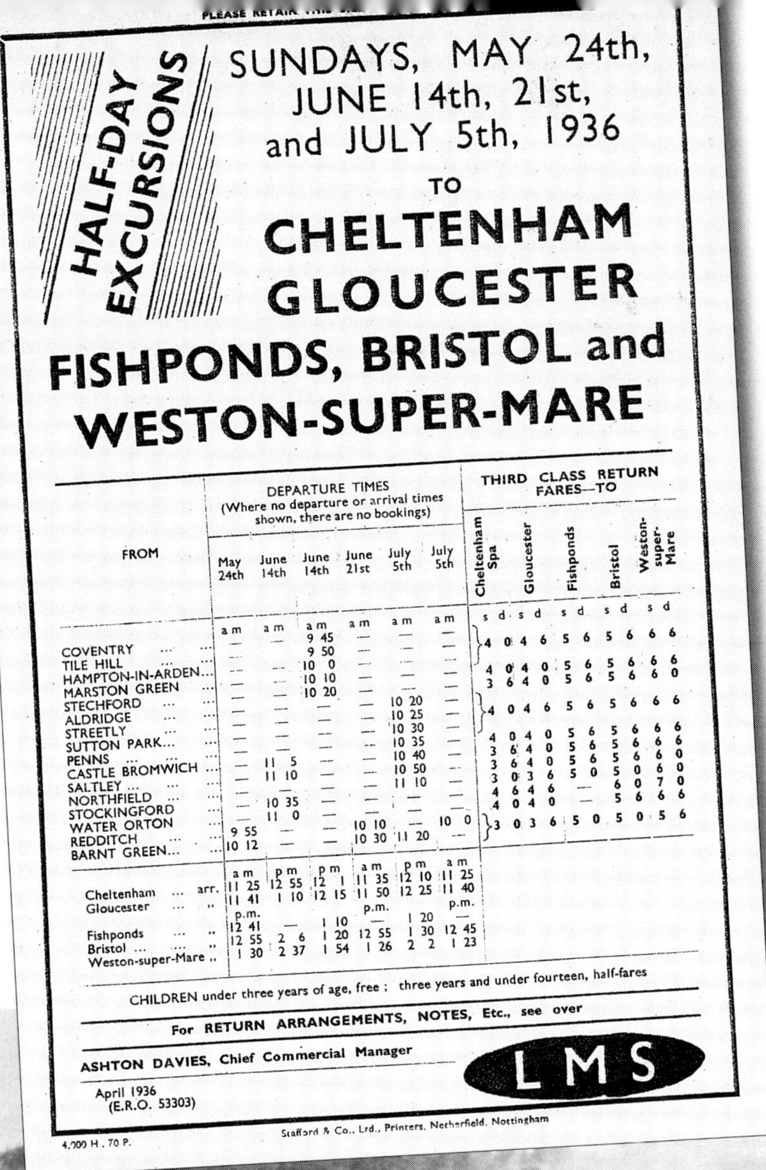

HALF-DAY EXCURSIONS

SUNDAYS, MAY 24th, JUNE 14th, 21st, and JULY 5th, 1936

TO

CHELTENHAM GLOUCESTER
FISHPONDS, BRISTOL and
WESTON-SUPER-MARE

DEPARTURE TIMES (Where no departure or arrival times shown, there are no bookings)

THIRD CLASS RETURN FARES—TO (s. d.)

FROM	May 24th	June 14th	June 14th	June 21st	July 5th	July 5th	Cheltenham Spa	Gloucester	Fishponds	Bristol	Weston-super-Mare
COVENTRY	—	—	9 45	—	—	—	4 0	4 6	5 6	5 6	6 6
TILE HILL	—	—	9 50	—	—	—	4 0	4 6	5 6	5 6	6 6
HAMPTON-IN-ARDEN	—	—	10 0	—	—	—	4 0	4 0	5 6	5 6	6 6
MARSTON GREEN	—	—	10 10	—	—	—	3 6	4 0	5 6	5 6	6 0
STECHFORD	—	—	10 20	—	10 20	—	4 0	4 6	5 6	5 6	6 6
ALDRIDGE	—	—	—	—	10 25	—	4 0	4 6	5 6	5 6	6 6
STREETLY	—	—	—	—	10 30	—	4 0	4 6	5 6	5 6	6 6
SUTTON PARK	—	—	—	—	10 35	—	4 0	4 0	5 6	5 6	6 6
PENNS	—	—	—	—	10 40	—	3 6	4 0	5 6	5 6	6 0
CASTLE BROMWICH	—	11 5	—	—	10 50	—	3 6	4 0	5 6	5 6	6 0
SALTLEY	—	11 10	—	—	11 10	—	3 0	3 6	5 0	5 0	6 0
NORTHFIELD	—	10 35	—	—	—	—	4 6	4 6	—	6 0	7 0
STOCKINGFORD	—	11 0	—	—	—	—	4 0	4 0	—	5 6	6 6
WATER ORTON	—	—	—	10 10	—	10 0	3 0	3 6	5 0	5 0	5 6
REDDITCH	9 55	—	—	10 30	11 20	—	3 0	3 6	5 0	5 0	5 6
BARNT GREEN	10 12	—	—	—	—	—	3 0	3 6	5 0	5 0	5 6

	a m	p m	p m	a m	p m	a m
Cheltenham ... arr.	11 25	12 55	12 1	11 35	12 10	11 25
Gloucester ... "	11 41	1 10	12 15	11 50	12 25	11 40
	p.m.			p.m.		p.m.
Fishponds ... "	12 41	—	1 10	—	1 20	—
Bristol ... "	12 55	2 6	1 20	12 55	1 30	12 45
Weston-super-Mare ..	1 30	2 37	1 54	1 26	2 2	1 23

CHILDREN under three years of age, free ; three years and under fourteen, half-fares

For **RETURN ARRANGEMENTS, NOTES, Etc.,** see over

ASHTON DAVIES, Chief Commercial Manager   **LMS**

April 1936
(E.R.O. 53303)

4,000 H . 70 P.

Stafford & Co., Ltd., Printers, Netherfield, Nottingham.

Left: Typical LMS leaflet advertising excursions available from the West Midlands down the Birmingham-Bristol line.

Below: **Hatherley, early 1960s.** Smartly turned-out 44910 hauls 'The City of Birmingham Holiday Express' past Hatherley signal box – note even the loco's lamps appear to be those kept for 'special' occasions, denoting the effort being made by the railway to give ordinary working folk a day out to remember. Millions of holidaymakers travelled down the line to their favoured West Country or South Coast resort for the annual fortnight's break over the years, while these specials with their distinctive headboards catered for day-trippers in August, with a different destination from Monday to Friday. Examples of similar trains were the 'City of Leicester Midland Holiday Express' with 45264 on 15 August 1962 and the 'Walsall & Wolverhampton Holiday Express' seen on 7 August 1963 with Shrewsbury shed's 45699 *Galatea* as motive power.   *R Stanton*

Above: **Barrow Road carriage sidings, 1956.** And here is 45699 *Galatea,* when it was a Bristol Barrow Road loco, standing in the sidings with empty stock for an express, judging from the engine's lamps. In autumn 1961 *Galatea* was displaced by diesels and transferred to Shrewsbury along with several other Barrow Road 'Jubilees'. Coaching stock for Midland trains starting or terminating at Temple Meads was stabled here. In the 1980s Avon County Council built a rail-connected waste disposal plant on the Barrow Road site. *Midland Railway Trust Ltd*

There were intermediate stations at Warmley, Bitton, and Weston, just outside Bath, when the line opened. Kelston for Saltford opened on 1 December 1869. A halt was placed at Oldland Common much later, 2 December 1935. Kelston succumbed to closure on and from 1 January 1949 and Weston from 21 September 1953, but the others survived until withdrawal of passenger trains on and from 7 March 1966.

At Bath, the temporary station of August 1869 was replaced by a permanent structure on 7 May 1870, with an imposing frontage, befitting this Spa town renowned for its architecture. Sometimes known as Bath Queen Square, the station did not officially change until June 1951, when BR renamed it Bath Green Park. Trains over the S&D into Bath commenced on 20 July 1874. But the S&D was in serious financial difficulty and the Midland Railway and London & South Western Railway agreed to lease it for 999 years from 1 November 1875. It thus became the Somerset & Dorset Joint Railway. Locomotives were then supplied by the Midland Railway, but were overhauled at the S&DJ's own works at Highbridge until its closure in 1930. Both the Midland and S&D had loco sheds at Bath, until amalgamated by the LMS. Weak bridges on the line from Mangotsfield to Bath limited the motive power used on the line until they were attended to in the 1930s.

Through carriages were run from Bournemouth as far afield as Newcastle. 'The Pines Express' was the most famous train traversing the Mangotsfield-Bath section and on over the S&D, often run in several parts at the height of the holiday season. So when it was diverted away from the line at the start of the winter timetable in September 1962, the bells started to toll for its eventual closure. This came for passenger traffic on and from 7 March 1966 – even this was delayed from early January 1966, the original closure date, which was postponed due to inadequate replacement road services. Goods traffic via Mangotsfield, particularly coal for Bath Gasworks, continued until May 1971.

After leaving Mangotsfield on the Bristol line, there was Staple Hill Tunnel, 514 yards long with the station just beyond. Another half-mile or so and the line passed Fishponds station and the sidings for locomotive manu-facturer The Avonside Engine Co. – which closed in the late 1920s The two miles of line down to Lawrence Hill Junction was steeply graded between 1 in 57 and 1 in 97, with a goodly stretch of 1 in 69, and many up trains were banked. Kingswood Junction was where the Avonmouth branch went off west, crossing viaducts and with tunnels at Montpelier and Clifton *en route*. Back on the main line from Lawrence Hill Junction, the Midland's Barrow Road loco shed was soon passed on the right, also its short branches to St Philips passenger and goods stations and Avonside Wharf. The joint lines into Temple Meads followed and terminating trains from Birmingham would probably arrive at the original Brunel terminus, while services continuing to the West Country such as the 'Devonian' would utilise the through platforms. The extremely modest passenger facilities at St Philips were used for local services to Bath until closure in September 1953, from when these train used Temple Meads. The magnificent Temple Meads had been a joint station between the MR, GWR and Bristol & Exeter Railway since 1878; long distance Midland trains tended to continue using the old Brunel train shed, which had an extension built during the years 1868-72 and became incorporated in the joint station. Originally of course the Brunel train shed had been solely broad gauge and used both by the GWR and Bristol & Gloucester Railway. From 1854 narrow gauge track was laid in to accommodate Midland Railway (ex Bristol & Gloucester) trains, of which there were at least five a day each way. The Bristol & Exeter Railway had its own station at right-angles to the Brunel train shed and as traffic increased, the set-up became unsatisfactory. The Midland obtained an Act in 1863 allowing a better connection with the Bristol & Exeter, but this was shelved in favour of an enlarged joint station for use by all three companies at Temple Meads. Broad gauge tracks in the station were removed in 1892 allowing some alterations of the layout, but this remained inadequate for the increasing traffic. In the 1930s a huge rebuilding was undertaken utilising govern-ment funds and the Temple Meads track layout became the one that remained for the rest of the steam era.

The accident at Charfield on 13 October 1928 around 5.15am rates as one of the major disasters in the history of British railways. The overnight mail and passenger train from Leeds to Bristol headed by Class 3 4-4-0 714 ran into a GWR goods train, the 9.15pm from Oxley Sidings, Wolverhampton, with 2-6-0 6381, which was reversing off the down main line into a dead-end siding to leave the road clear for the express. But with fatal consequences the latter ran past a signal set at danger and smashed into the goods wagons at more than sixty miles an hour. Further devastation was caused because there was another goods train coming through on the up main – and all this occurred under a bridge. Add in the fact that the coaches were built of wood and lit by gas, which was rapidly set alight by fire falling from the engine, and the result was that sixteen people died – including two children who were very badly burnt and have never been identified. Loco 714, whose driver and fireman miraculously survived, was so badly damaged that it was scrapped.

Above: **Hatherley, early 1960s.** Strings of light engines returning to Saltley after working down on extra coal trains were a particularly common feature on Sundays. Up to five locos were coupled together, sometimes of five different classes, but here there are three 4Fs trundling northwards past Hatherley signal box. The leading one is Saltley's 44263; this depot had the largest 4F allocation on BR.
R Stanton

Cheltenham Lansdown station, 7 July 1962. The winds of change are evident as diesel D86 heads a part-fitted Bristol to Water Orton freight. The motive power is modern, but the wagons and signals are from the steam age. Diesels started working some of the more important freights on the Birmingham-Bristol route from November 1961, following their introduction on passenger services in June that year. This end of Lansdown station was altered in 1965 when the up and down platforms were extended to accommodate longer trains; prior to this, such trains had to draw up. It also enabled Cheltenham-Paddington trains to start here, sounding the death knell for the ex-GW St James and Malvern Road stations, which closed to passenger traffic at the start of 1966.

Michael Mensing

GRADIENT PROFILE – CHELTENHAM TO BRISTOL AND BATH

MANGOTSFIELD N. JC.–BATH
(M. P's. UP (WEST) SIDE FROM ZERO AT LONDON RD. JC., DERBY, VIA WHITACRE AND CAMP HILL

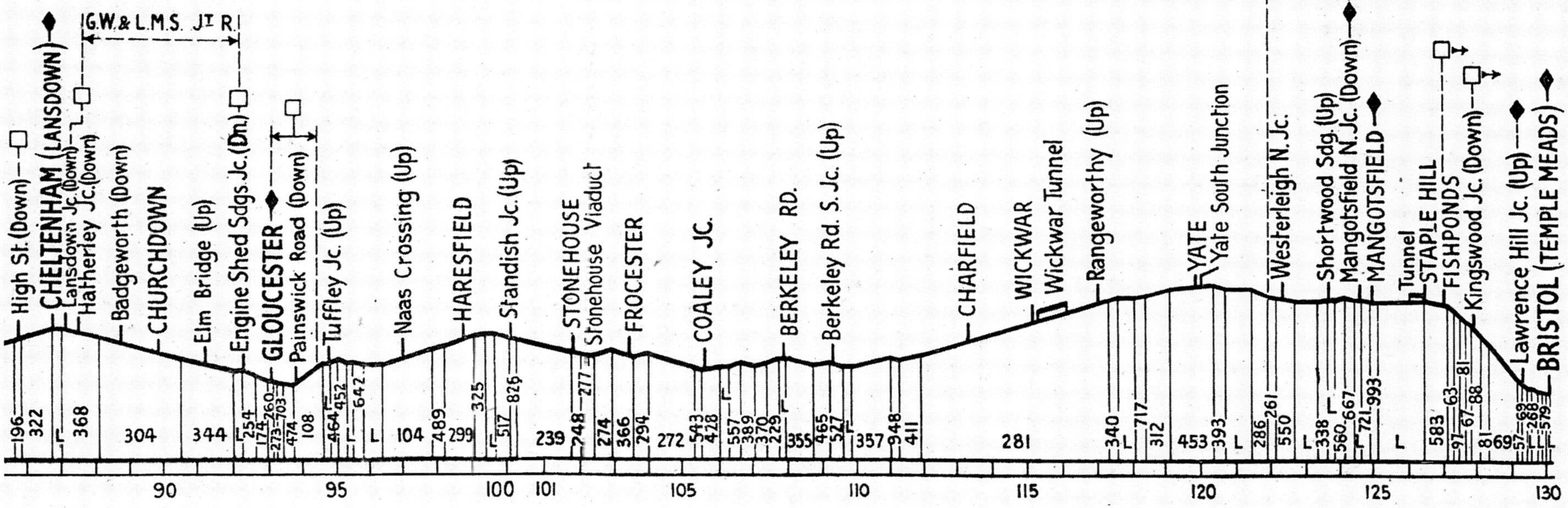

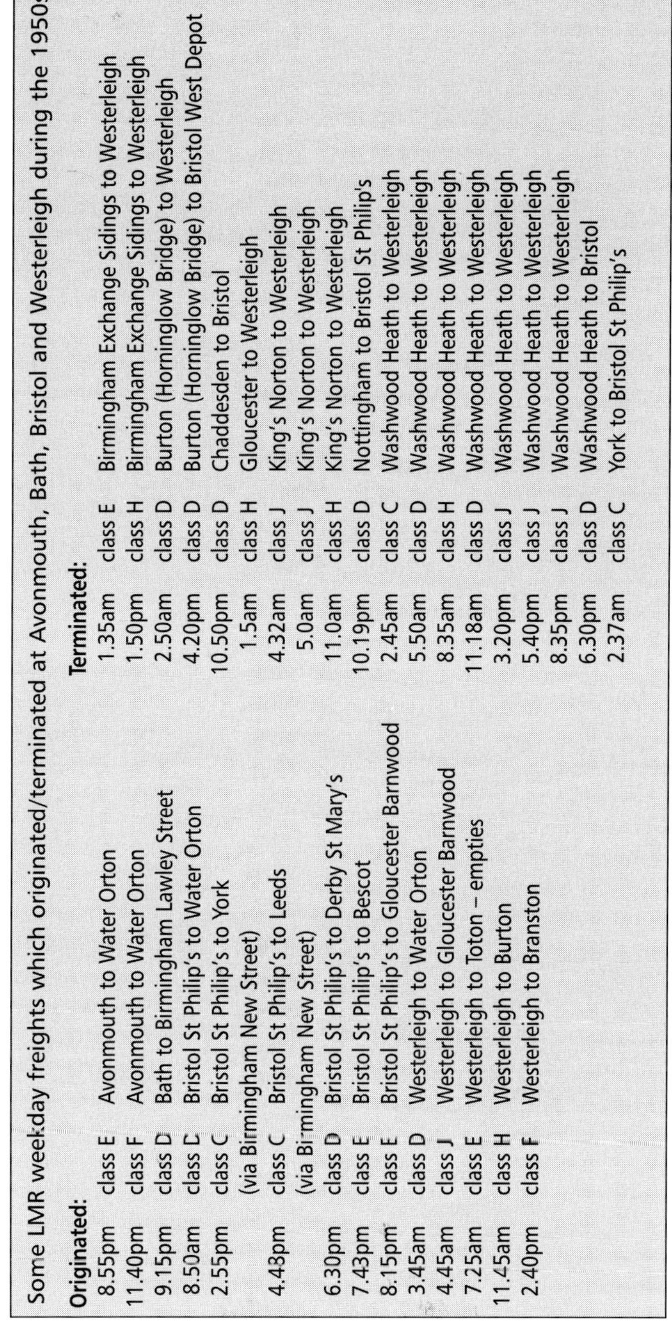

Some LMR weekday freights which originated/terminated at Avonmouth, Bath, Bristol and Westerleigh during the 1950s

Originated:

8.55pm	class E	Avonmouth to Water Orton
11.40pm	class F	Avonmouth to Water Orton
9.15pm	class D	Bath to Birmingham Lawley Street
8.50am	class D	Bristol St Philip's to Water Orton
2.55pm	class C	Bristol St Philip's to York
	(via Birmingham New Street)	
4.48pm	class C	Bristol St Philip's to Leeds
	(via Birmingham New Street)	
6.30pm	class D	Bristol St Philip's to Derby St Mary's
7.43pm	class E	Bristol St Philip's to Bescot
8.15pm	class E	Bristol St Philip's to Gloucester Barnwood
3.45am	class D	Westerleigh to Water Orton
4.45am	class J	Westerleigh to Gloucester Barnwood
7.25am	class E	Westerleigh to Toton – empties
11.45am	class H	Westerleigh to Burton
2.40pm	class F	Westerleigh to Branston

Terminated:

1.35am	class E	Birmingham Exchange Sidings to Westerleigh
1.50pm	class H	Birmingham Exchange Sidings to Westerleigh
2.50am	class D	Burton (Horninglow Bridge) to Westerleigh
4.20pm	class D	Burton (Horninglow Bridge) to Bristol West Depot
10.50pm	class D	Chaddesden to Bristol
1.5am	class H	Gloucester to Westerleigh
4.32am	class J	King's Norton to Westerleigh
5.0am	class J	King's Norton to Westerleigh
11.0am	class H	King's Norton to Westerleigh
10.19pm	class D	Nottingham to Bristol St Philip's
2.45am	class C	Washwood Heath to Westerleigh
5.50am	class D	Washwood Heath to Westerleigh
8.35am	class H	Washwood Heath to Westerleigh
11.18am	class D	Washwood Heath to Westerleigh
3.20pm	class J	Washwood Heath to Westerleigh
5.40pm	class J	Washwood Heath to Westerleigh
8.35pm	class J	Washwood Heath to Westerleigh
6.30pm	class D	Washwood Heath to Bristol
2.37am	class C	York to Bristol St Philip's

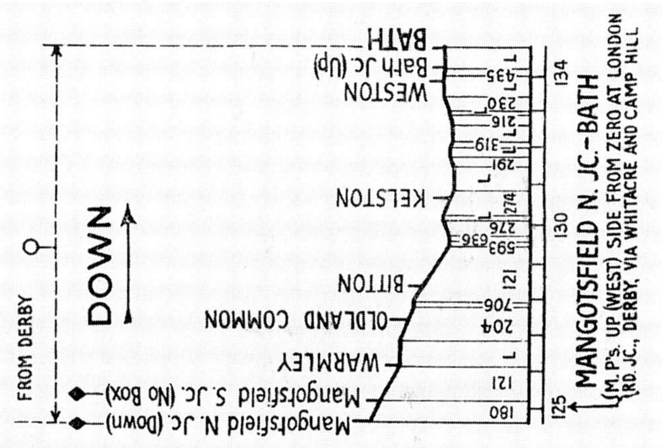

Left, above: **Cheltenham station, 1900s.** This is a super portrait of Johnson 'Spinner' 4-2-2 133 at Lansdown. Built in 1892, with 7'6" driving wheels, 133 was renumbered 649 in 1907. The MSWJ bay came into operation in January 1900. In 1903 through MR carriages were run from Sheffield, departing at 11.32am, arriving at Southampton at 5.54pm and possibly the MSWJ loco in the bay is waiting to couple up to them when the MR train has departed.

Lens of Sutton

Left, below: **Cheltenham station, mid-1900s.** Kirtley double framed 0-6-0 688 stands on the down line at Lansdown sometime between 1903 and 1907, when it was renumbered 2681. Built at Derby Works in 1869, the loco survived until 1925. Classified 1F, there were as many as 449 of these curved frame Kirtleys at the grouping in 1923, so they were a familiar sight for many years. The train obscures the 'Cheltenham' station sign which included the legend 'Change here for Paris' – via the MSWJ to Southampton.

Rail Archive Stephenson

Above: **Lansdown Junction.** Class 2 4-4-0 513 leaves Cheltenham station and traverses the junction with a down express composed of Midland celestory stock. 513 carries a Bristol shed plate and has a canvas back to the cab, a form of 'blackout' used during the First World War to hide the glare from the fire. Class 3 4-4-0s dealt with the heaviest express passengers on the route, but the Class 2s did the rest, including trains to Bath, as the Class 3s were not allowed on the line from Mangotsfield. This picture shows Lansdown Junction when there were just two tracks to Gloucester with the box dating from May 1914. The lines curving off to the right behind the train are those of the GWR to Malvern Road, the Honeybourne line and St James.

A B MacLeod / NRM

The speed of all trains was restricted – to 20mph over the curves through Lansdown station; and 40mph on all lines through Lansdown Junction.

Left, above: **Lansdown Junction, 9 April 1946.** 'Black Five' 4873 departs with train M937, including a rather venerable looking carriage behind the engine. The train is signalled to take the down main line towards Gloucester. The signals 'off' on the right of the gantry indicate a train is due out of the GWR's Malvern Road station onto the down relief line. Prior to August 1942, there was only one down – and one up – line between Cheltenham and Gloucester leading to severe delays on this very busy section. *E R Morten*

Left, below: **Lansdown Junction, 14 September 1955.** Worcester shed's 4-6-0 6950 *Kingsthorpe Hall* heads home on a local passenger train at the junction as it was after the wartime remodelling. The lines diverging left are for Andoversford. Before nationalisation, the lines to Gloucester were joint between the GWR and LMS; the GWR was responsible for maintenance from here to just west of Churchdown station, with the LMS looking after the lines from there to close to Tramway Junction, Gloucester. The signal box seen came into use in July 1942 and controlled something over 300 movements on an average weekday; the shell still exists. The old box, seen in a previous picture, was closed down and demolished. *E R Morten*

Above: **Cloddy Bridge, 28 March 1956.** The four tracks from Lansdown Junction, with the signal box in the background, are shown as Bath-based 45440 takes a fitted freight, possibly the 11.18am Washwood Heath-Westerleigh, out of Cheltenham. Upon widening to four tracks here, a footbridge was erected in place of the previous crossing and was a favourite place for taking pictures. 45440 – and 44917 – were the last two 'Black Fives' based at Bath, being transferred away in June 1958, though of course many members of the class still worked into Green Park. *E R Morten*

Above: **Hatherley,1930s.** Compound 1030 of Bristol Barrow Road shed is captured on film at Hatherley with an express. Both pictures on this page illustrate the days when there were just two tracks from Cheltenham to Gloucester.

C F H Oldham

Below: **Badgeworth.** Another picture from LMS days finds a train heading north between Churchdown and Cheltenham – bound for London! This is one of the famous Fyffes banana trains from Avonmouth Docks to London Somers Town which was routed via Gloucester, Ashchurch, Broom Junction, the erstwhile Stratford-upon-Avon & Midland Junction Railway, Olney, Bedford and the Midland main line to London. The perishable nature of the goods meant these were express trains, carrying class 'C' head codes and 'for which lower classified services must be kept clear.' The loco is Midland 4F 3875, in pre-1928 livery, which worked to Broom, where a reversal was necessary, so a fresh loco took the train from there. An even longer way round from Bristol to Somers Town was taken by a regular empty coaching stock train – often 20 vehicles with an '8F' – which travelled via Birmingham and Leicester, a journey of 226 miles.

D H Haines / HMRS

Badgeworth. The four track era finds Saltley's 8F 2-8-0 48220 on a down goods on 4 November 1961 and 44775, also of Saltley, heading north on 9 August 1958 with M222, 9.50am Weston-Super-Mare to Birmingham New Street and overtaking shedmate 44571 hauling a brake van. The 4F is most likely going to Evesham to work the afternoon Water Orton goods. This section was quadrupled in August 1942 and the signal box seen here opened a month earlier, but was relatively short-lived, closing in October 1952, though the structure survived for several more years. *B W L Brooksbank*

Above: **Churchdown.** Approaching together are 'Jubilee' 45626 *Seychelles* on a down express and an unidentified 84XX 0-6-0PT on a local from Cheltenham St James. Though it might be rather unequal in this instance, WR and LMR engines often raced each other between Cheltenham and Gloucester. The majority of trains which stopped at Churchdown were from St James, though a couple of Birmingham New Street services also called here each day.   *R K Blencowe collection*

Below: **Churchdown, 8 August 1960.** No doubt as to where this picture was taken. Churchdown had been a joint GWR/LMS station, but passed solely to the Western Region shortly after nationalisation. The station had no sidings, so goods traffic was brought by road from Cheltenham or Gloucester. The box is another wartime addition, opened in June 1942, replacing an earlier one and survived in use until February 1967. It is situated between the up relief and up main lines.

H B Priestley

Above: **Churchdown, 9 August 1958.** 4F 44526 trundles through on a down freight. The two lines between the platforms are the up and down main. The platforms were widened in March 1944 to allow trains on the up and down relief lines to stop here. *R J Essery collection*

Below: **Elm Bridge, early 1960s.** The box was opened on 29 January 1940, but is not a wartime-type structure. It was approximately half-way between the boxes at Churchdown and Engine Shed Junction. Up and down goods lines came into use from here to Engine Shed Sidings on 3 May 1942, being made relief lines – usable by passenger trains – in July 1942. Elm Bridge did not work on Sundays and closed altogether on 5 June 1965. *R Stanton*

Barnwood, 18 July 1962. With Engine Shed Junction box just visible behind the big signal gantry, 5089 *Westminster Abbey* brings the down 'Cornishman' past the loco depot, while a diesel shunter potters in the goods yard. A 'Peak' diesel and three 9F 2-10-0s are visible in the shed yard; 9Fs were too long to be turned on the roundhouse turntable, so were stabled in the open. From September 1962 the 'Cornishman' was diverted from starting at Wolverhampton Low Level and travelling via Birmingham Snow Hill to commencing at Sheffield and coming down through New Street; and it was rostered for diesel haulage.   *B J Ashworth*

Barnwood shed. The loco depot opened in July 1894 and replaced the earlier one which was on the site of the new Midland passenger station opened in 1896. The first picture dated July 1959 shows, from left: coal stage; roundhouse; former workshops. Behind the engines a tin shed covers the wheel drop, utilised by locos from quite a wide area. The third loco in the line-up is 2P 4-4-0 40489. The second photo displays Beyer Garratt 47972 on 22 October 1955. The type was not that uncommon at Gloucester. *Rail Archive Stephenson / F W Shuttleworth*

The allocation at 22B Gloucester in January 1948			
4-4-0 2P	3	0-6-0 3F	13
4-4-0 4P	8	0-6-0 4F	14
0-4-0T 0F	2	0-6-0T 3F	4
0-6-0T 1F	3	0-4-4T 1P	4
2-6-0 5F	1	0-6-0 2F	1
		Total	**53**

Left, above: **Gloucester avoiding line, 16 July 1966.** The line from Gloucester South Junction to Engine Shed Junction enabled trains to bypass Gloucester Eastgate station. 44780 goes north at Engine Shed Junction with an empty stock train, off the avoiding line onto the Cheltenham route from Eastgate and Central, which comes in from the right in this picture. By this date, steam workings were pretty rare at Gloucester and within a couple of months, were virtually extinct.
N E Preedy

Left, below: **Gloucester avoiding line, 8 August 1964.** Having taken the avoiding line at Gloucester South 92160 blasts northwards on train 1N01 from Weston-Super-Mare to Sheffield. 9Fs started appearing on passenger trains on the Birmingham–Bristol route in 1957 and as the years rolled by, they sometimes worked regular expresses and locals, not just summer reliefs.
R K Blencowe collection

Above: **Gloucester avoiding line.** While passenger trains using the avoiding line were mainly summer reliefs, freight traffic was always heavy. BR Standard 78005 coasts along on an unfitted freight. Plenty of freights stopped for water and a crew change at Gloucester South.
R K Blencowe collection

Whistle codes for Birmingham-Bristol trains using the Gloucester avoiding line: on the down – one long, one short, one long when passing through Cleeve station (north of Cheltenham); on the up – one long, two short at Berkeley Road Junction.

Above: **Gloucester avoiding line, 18 April 1963.** Reduced to mundane work by dieselisation, 'Jubilee' 45676 *Codrington* passes the 'T' sidings footbridge on a southbound freight. Gloucester South Junction and its signal box lie ahead of the train.

B J Ashworth

Below: **Gloucester South Junction, 21 August 1965.** 44808 has the 10.05 Wolverhampton Low Level-Kingswear. By summer 1965 ex-LMS and BR Standards, including 'Britannias' predominated on these summer Saturday workings which came down from Birmingham on the Honeybourne line, though ex-GW types still appeared, usually bereft of nameplates.

B J Ashworth

Above: **Tramway Junction.** Going back on the route into Gloucester's stations, Barnwood-based 3F 43258 (seen at Cheltenham in 1933 on one of the back cover pictures) passes the box on an unfitted goods. Barnwood sidings can be glimpsed between the box and train, while the line from Swindon comes in on the right.

B W L Brooksbank / Initial Photographs

Below: **Tramway Junction.** Rail movements here were always very busy, holding up lots of road traffic. Apart from trains to and from the Birmingham, Bristol, Swindon and South Wales routes, there were constant shunting movements across the crossing. Behind is Horton Road engine shed, the GWR's depot in Gloucester.

R K Blencowe collection

Above: **Gloucester station, 11 April 1896.** This is the old Midland Railway passenger station in Gloucester and the picture at the terminus is reputed to show the last train to use it, the 7.40am slow to Birmingham with a 2-4-0. It was inconvenient to have through trains arriving at and departing from a terminus, so a new through station was needed. But history repeats itself, with Birmingham-Bristol trains today having to run in and reverse out.   *R & CHS*

Below and right, above: **Gloucester stations.** These two pictures contrast the exteriors of the old Midland station and its replacement, not to mention the differences in road transport between the first shot, on 11 April 1896 and the second, in October 1953.
R & CHS; Mowat collection

Above: **Gloucester station, c.1910.** Class 3 4-4-0 757 provides a fine portrait on an up express. This class of loco was the most powerful motive power on the Birmingham-Bristol line until the advent of Class 4 Compounds in the 1920s. The carriage is third class, but of a more comfortable standard than other railways. The Midland was the first to introduce third class accommodation on all trains, in 1872, and have upholstered seats and lavatories in third class carriages. There were many through carriage workings up to the First World War such as Bristol to Heysham and Stranraer to name just two.

R S Carpenter collection

Above: **Gloucester station, 13 March 1924.** It is now the LMS era but 4-4-0 426 still displays Midland Railway livery as it waits in the carriage sidings. 426, originally constructed in 1896, was still a regular on the route in the 1950s when it was allocated to Bristol Barrow Road, being withdrawn in November 1957. 4-4-0s were a feature for many years, the last ones did not finally disappear from Barnwood shed until 1962, though latterly in store.   *R S Carpenter collection*

Below: **Gloucester station, 1938.** The powerful and distinctive Compound 4-4-0s were built by the Midland Railway from 1902 but it was the mid-1920s before they started regular work between Birmingham and Bristol. Bournville shed's 1073 poses alongside an unfamiliar visitor – an Armstrong Whitworth 3-car articulated diesel unit – perhaps the shape of things to come….

Midland Railway Trust Ltd

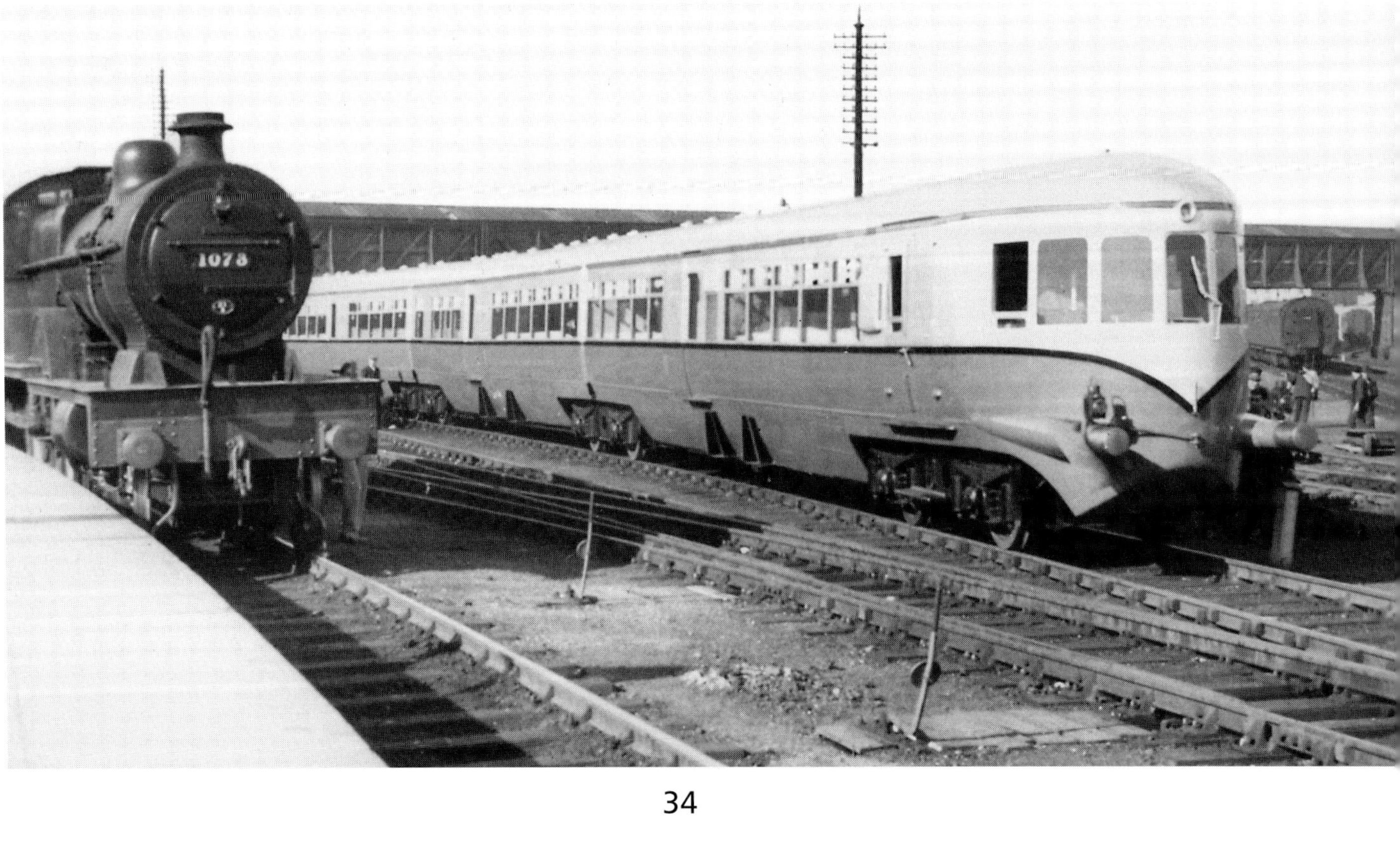

Above: **Gloucester Eastgate station.** A quiet period enables this photo from the down side to show the sweeping curve of the platform.
Joe Moss collection / R S Carpenter

Below: **Gloucester Eastgate station.** This view reveals the main signal box, located at the northern end of the up platform. The footbridge between Eastgate and Central stations can be seen in the background. The differently styled water towers for the Midland and Great Western are prominent in the centre, while the lines to Central are over to the right as is the Western goods shed.
Joe Moss collection / R S Carpenter

Gloucester Eastgate, 12 August 1959. LMS-built Compound 41123 shunts the carriage sidings. It was allocated to Barnwood in May 1957 when two or three others of the class were still there, but it became the last one at Gloucester, withdrawn in December 1959. Barnwood had the last Midland Railway Compound to be in service, 41025, withdrawn in January 1953. It was still working Birmingham-Bristol stoppers in November 1952, but was cut up at Derby immediately upon withdrawal.

S Rickard collection

Above: **Gloucester Midland Goods, 13 April 1962.** Another old-stager, 3F 43754 shunts the Midland goods shed sidings. The former passenger terminus was located just off the picture on the right. 43754 was a long-time resident at Barnwood shed. It fell to this engine to work the last passenger trains on the Ashchurch-Upton line on 12 August 1961.

B W L Brooksbank / Initial Photographs

Below: **Gloucester Eastgate, 2 December 1961.** Looking north from the goods sidings presents a typically busy scene. There is a passenger train on the far right in the down platform. A carriage shunt is taking place near Passenger Station signal box, while a BR Standard Class 5, probably one of the Barnwood trio of 73091, 73092 and 73093, stands partly on the yard turntable – this was longer than the one in Barnwood roundhouse, so came in useful for turning engines such as 9Fs. A clean 'Castle' over on the Western side looks ready for action, with steam to spare. Horton Road shed is visible through the steam and smoke.

B J Ashworth

Above: **Gloucester Eastgate, 12 August 1959.** Burton- based 'Crab' 2-6-0 42799 waits in the up side bay with a local train for Birmingham. The goods yard can be seen on the right, with the covered footbridge prominent across the picture.   *S Rickard collection*

Below: **Gloucester Eastgate, 12 August 1959.** The platform buildings are seen to good effect as station pilot 41123 waits in the down side platform 3 to remove the empty stock of a recently-arrived local passenger train. 41123 was in the twilight of its life but was still noted as far away as York in this month on an express from the Sheffield direction.   *S Rickard collection*

Above: **Gloucester Eastgate, 12 August 1959.** A very busy scene – the down platform is occupied by 73065 on a local terminating here – the one whose stock will be removed by 41123 – 45519 *Lady Godiva* on an express and 44272 in Upper Yard.
S Rickard collection

Below: **Gloucester.** This view from the Midland station up platform towards Bristol shows the elevated signal box at Barton Street. A train is signalled out of the Upper Yard onto the main line. Just beyond the box, the right-hand line goes off to Gloucester Docks.
Author's collection

Above: **Barton Street, 12 October 1961.** The 'Cornishman' passes, hauled by 5031 *Totnes Castle* a regular engine on this turn. From 1928, a GWR 4-6-0 worked the 'Devonian' out of Eastgate on Saturdays plus Fridays at a later date, and up to 1939, 'Saints', 'Halls', 'Stars' and 'Castles' could be observed pounding up to Tuffley Junction. *B J Ashworth*

Inset: **California Crossing.** Next on the route, just 18 chains from Barton Street, was this old Midland Railway box, which is now preserved in working order at the North Gloucestershire Railway, Toddington. The name 'California' was used for this district, allegedly due to its 'Wild West' nature in earlier times! *M A King*

Above: **Gloucester Docks lines, 12 May 1961.** The line behind California box goes to Gloucester Docks, which is where Somerset & Dorset 2-8-0 53806 is heading on a transfer freight. 53806 is an unusual loco to be seen on the branch, but it had just received attention to a hot box at Barnwood shed and the Docks turn was often used for running-in locos after repair.

B J Ashworth

Below and overleaf: **Gloucester Docks lines.** Although not visible from the main line, it is difficult to leave Gloucester without a quick look at the docks, at least on the Midland side. Two Deeley tanks were allocated to Barnwood until the end of steam on the docks jobs and both are illustrated: 41535 at the Southgate Street entrance on 9 April 1962 and, overleaf, 41537 at Llanthony Swing Bridge on 10 November 1961. Also shown is a wagon constructed by the Gloucester Railway Carriage & Wagon Company Limited, whose works was connected to the dock lines. The company's products were exported all over the world and provided traffic for the Birmingham-Bristol line for decades.

B J Ashworth (2); HMRS

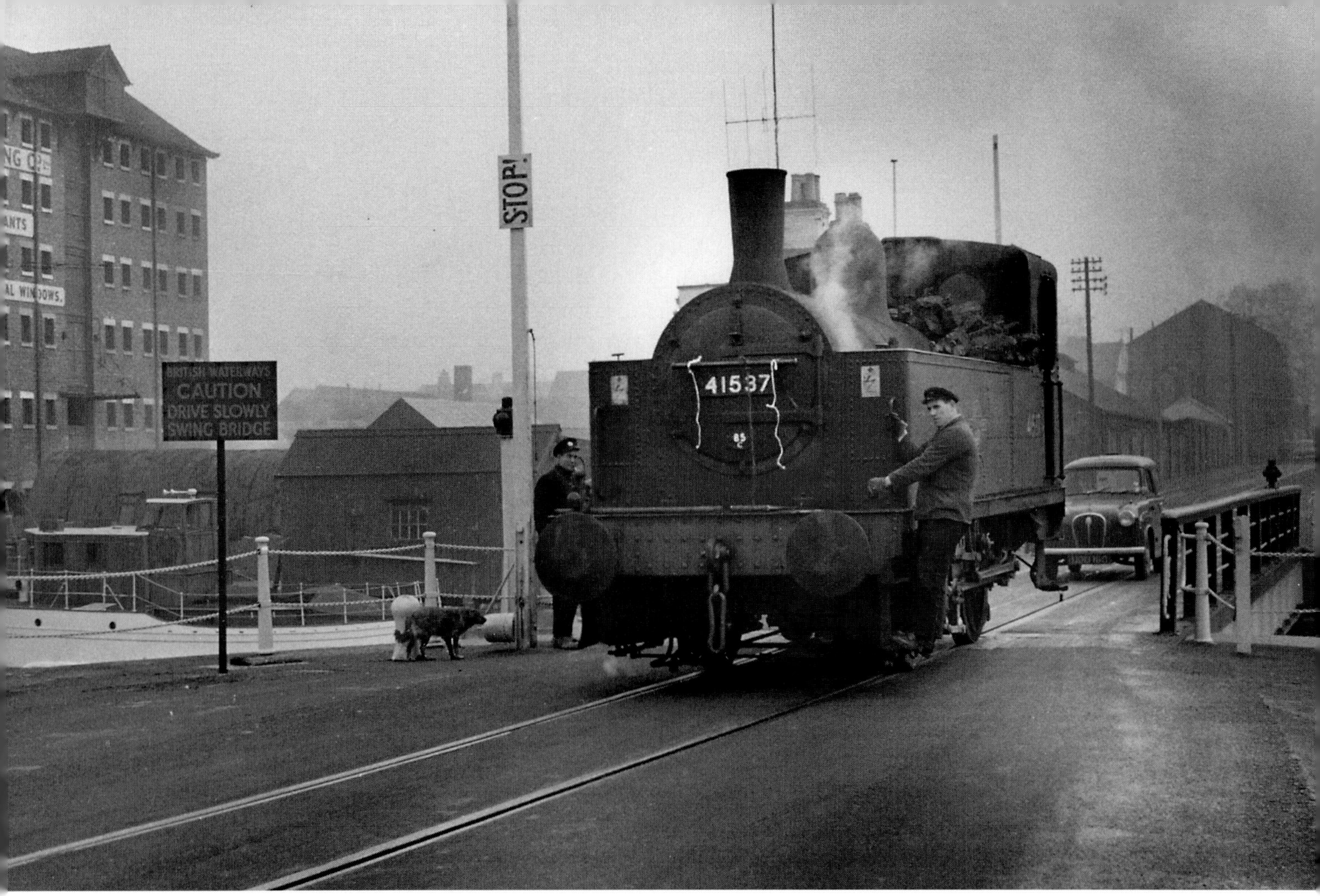
STOP!
BRITISH WATERWAYS
CAUTION
DRIVE SLOWLY
SWING BRIDGE
41537

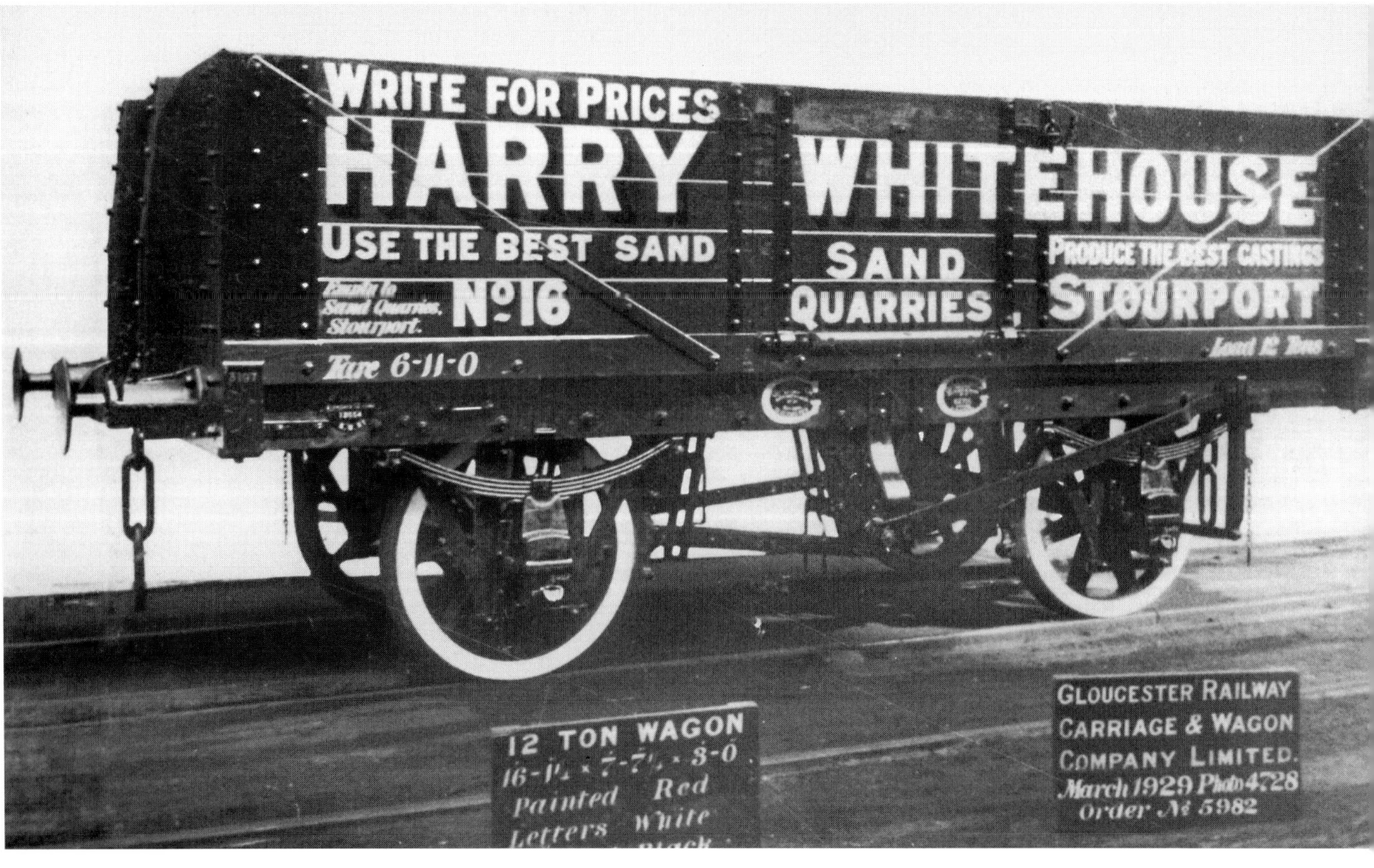
WRITE FOR PRICES
HARRY WHITEHOUSE
USE THE BEST SAND
SAND QUARRIES
PRODUCE THE BEST CASTINGS
Empty to Sand Quarries, Stourport.
No 16
STOURPORT
Tare 6-11-0
Load 12 Tons
12 TON WAGON
16-1½ x 7-7½ x 3-0
Painted Red
Letters White
GLOUCESTER RAILWAY
CARRIAGE & WAGON
COMPANY LIMITED.
March 1929 Photo 4728
Order No 5982

Above: **Tuffley, 12 August 1959.** *Totnes Castle* has plenty of steam as it runs towards Tuffley Junction with the down 'Cornishman'. There was a climb at 1 in 108 for a mile and a half out of Gloucester through the suburbs to Tuffley Junction and a banking loco was available if required. The reporting number chalked on the loco's smokebox refers to a working on an earlier date; the 'Cornishman' was number 825 at the time. *S Rickard collection*

Below: **Tuffley, 12 August 1959.** 'Jubilee' 45682 *Trafalgar* curves away from Tuffley Junction on an up express. The lines on the left were used by trains going to Gloucester Central and for the avoiding line. *S Rickard collection*

Above: **Tuffley, 12 August 1959.** Barnwood stalwart 43645 trundles through Tuffley Junction, possibly on the Stroud and Nailsworth branch freight. *S Rickard collection*

Below: **Tuffley, 12 August 1959.** Tuffley Junction box is in view as 0-6-0T 47422 brings a trip working with a respectable number of wagons from Quedgeley to Upper Yard and Barnwood Sidings. The branch to Hempsted goes off to the right by the box. The working time table noted: 'These trips must be given special attention…and… must have preference over all other trains except passenger, parcels and 'C' 'D' and 'E' code freight trains.' *S Rickard collection*

Above: **Naas Crossing to Haresfield, late 1940s.** Barnwood 4F 43846 has charge of a down mixed freight in early BR days. The loco, which is fitted with an original type tall chimney and dome, has its new owner's name in full on the tender, receiving its BR identity in November 1948. This four track section ran from Tuffley Junction to Standish Junction, just over five miles. The two Midland tracks are nearest the camera, with two Western lines on the right.

W Dendy

Below: **Near Haresfield, 29 July 1961.** Ivatt 2-6-0 43122 heads the 1.18pm Saturdays only Gloucester-Bristol stopper. The train called at all stations except Frocester and was due into Temple Meads at 2.43pm.   *B W L Brooksbank*

Haresfield. A couple of views looking north at this wayside station. Although there is probably 50 or more years separating the two photos, time seems to have stood still. The platforms only served the Midland tracks here, there were none on the GW side. In 1962 three up trains stopped Monday-Friday, with one setting down only, while there were five down stoppers, with one setting down only. *Author's collection*

Standish Junction, 2 October 1960. This was where the Midland and Great Western parted company, the former heading for Bristol and Bath, while the latter went to Swindon. The view of WD 90448 shows it crossing from the GW lines to the Midland lines on a down freight, while a 4F on an engineering train occupies the up line by the signal box.

H C Casserley

Above: **Standish Junction, 8 August 1964.** The Saturdays only 2.30pm Paignton-Wolverhampton traverses Standish with 5026 *Criccieth Castle*. This train did not stop in Gloucester, and went via South Junction. Standish Junction layout had remained pretty much the same since 1908, but big changes were about to take place. *B J Ashworth*

Below: **Standish Junction, 4 November 1964.** A double junction was installed at Standish over the weekend of 24-26 October 1964, and enabled, for example, Cheltenham-Paddington trains to utilise Midland tracks out of Gloucester before crossing to the Swindon line here. Using Eastgate station in Gloucester instead of Central did away with the need for reversal and change of locos there. The new arrangement is illustrated in this picture as a London train crosses to the Swindon line. *B J Ashworth*

Above: **Stonehouse, c.1923.** Stonehouse was blessed with two stations – one on the Bristol and one on the Swindon line. The Midland station, known as Stonehouse Bristol Road in BR days, is seen in a view taken from the up platform, presenting a neat, solid image.   *Stations UK*

Below: **Stonehouse, 28 May 1947.** As can be seen on the station name board, Stonehouse was the junction for the Stroud and Nailsworth lines. Here is 0-4-4T 1330 – later BR 58051 and retaining round top firebox and Salter safety valves – at the branch platform. The passenger service on the branches had just two years life left, ceasing early in the BR era, June 1949.   *R J Buckley, Initial Photographs*

Above: **Stonehouse, 30 June 1965.** The freight service on the branches however continued well into the 1960s and 44264 is pictured at the old branch platform, not long before the end of steam on the working.　　*Author's collection*

Below: **Stonehouse, 1884.** South of the station was viaduct no.85 which is shown under construction, with a Midland 0-6-0 on a works train. This structure replaced a Brunel timber viaduct of 1844. Until 1927, when the viaduct was replaced by an embankment, heavier locos such as Midland Compound 4-4-0s and Great Western 4-6-0s were not allowed on the line; class 3 4-4-0s on the Midland and 'County' 4-4-0s on the GWR were the typical power on their respective Birmingham-Bristol expresses. At the time of writing in 2003, the embankment is slipping and is undergoing remedial work.　　*Author's collection*

Above: **Frocester.** Less than two miles on from Stonehouse was the small wayside station at Frocester. Opened in July 1844, it survived until total closure to both passenger and goods traffic in December 1961. Note the wagon turntable outside the goods shed. From 1918 until April 1924 there was a branch from slightly north of Frocester to gravel pits at Frampton-on-Severn. The line was built by German prisoners of war. *D Ibbotson*

Below: **Coaley Junction, 18 August 1932.** Another two miles on was Coaley Junction, originally named Dursley Junction, where the short branch to Cam and Dursley turned south from the down side of the main line. The branch had five or six passenger trains on weekdays, with a couple more on Saturdays; these finished in September 1962, although freight continued until the end of October 1966. *Mowat collection*

Coaley Junction. Midland IF 0-6-0T tanks worked the branch for years and 1720 is illustrated in late LMS days, 28 May 1947. Around a decade later, 0-6-0PT 1605 had taken over, along with some of its classmates. Tender engines were also seen, usually Midland 0-6-0s, but towards the end of the passenger service, Ivatt 2-6-0s 46526 and 46527 were regulars. 46527 is seen on 7 July 1962 running round its single coach at Coaley after arrival with the 7.5pm from Dursley.

R J Buckley, Initial Photographs; Michael Mensing

Berkeley Road. The next station was at Berkeley Road, where the line to Sharpness was opened by the Midland in 1875. The independent Severn & Wye Railway and the Severn Bridge Co. carried the line across the River Severn to Lydney from 1879. These two companies were jointly taken over by the GWR and MR in 1894, with passenger and freight services worked by GWR engines based at Lydney shed. MR locos retained the workings from Berkeley Road to Sharpness Docks.

The two views show the island platform building, of Midland Railway design, in November 1964, with the Sharpness branch curving off; and the Brunel-designed Bristol & Gloucester Railway goods shed, in 1960.

Author's collection; D Ibbotson

Left, above: **Berkeley Road, early 1890s.** The Severn & Wye Railway's 0-6-0T *Friar Tuck* and Gloucester RCW coach wait with the branch train. Built by the Avonside Engine Co of Fishponds, Bristol in 1870, the loco was taken over by the Midland Railway in 1895. *LGRP*

Left, below: **Berkeley Road, 9 August 1947.** Motor-fitted 0-6-0PT 2080 await departure on the 6.35pm to Lydney Town, due there at 7.4pm. The last LMS and GWR time tables, from 6 October 1947, show a service of eight trains each way Monday-Friday, one less on Saturdays and none on Sundays. 2080 was an interesting loco, having been rebuilt in 1930 with 5'6'' driving wheels, fitted for auto train working and initially renumbered 5400. In the background, LMS Compound 1073 departs with the 5.15pm Bristol-Birmingham stopper. A snippet about 1073 – it was in collision with 'Jubilee' 5621 *Northern Rhodesia* at Barrow Road loco in May 1943, resulting in damage and derailment. *W A Camwell*

Above: **Sharpness, 12 March 1950.** A quick glimpse here shows venerable 'Dean Goods' 0-6-0 2414 on the 8.25am Cardiff-Bristol, diverted via the Severn Bridge, seen in the background, due to engineering work in the Severn Tunnel. On this train, 2414 worked through to Bristol via Berkeley Road South Junction. It returned on the 12.57pm Bristol-Cardiff. 'Dean Goods' from Lydney shed and elsewhere were used over the bridge due to their light axle load, though later in the 1950s larger GW locos, 4300 Class 'Moguls', were permitted. If the bridge had not been fatally damaged by a barge in October 1960, it would have been strengthened to take heavier engines, but the accident led to its immediate closure and subsequent demolition. *T J Edgington*

Overleaf: **Charfield.** A couple of views at the station looking north. This was the scene of the horrific accident on 13 October 1928. Class 3 4-4-0 714 was scrapped as a result, though the GWR loco 2-6-0 6381 survived. The close-up, taken in November 1964, shows the original Bristol & Gloucester Railway up side building.

Author's collection; R J Essery collection

Above: **Wickwar, c1910**. Famous for its cider, this was the next station on the main line. The photo shows the main buildings, located on the down side, which date from the opening of the Bristol-Gloucester line in 1844. Just beyond the station is the cider works and a little further on is Wickwar tunnel.   *Lens of Sutton*

Below: **Wickwar, 6 August 1956**. BR Standard 4-6-0 73069, of Leeds Holbeck shed, pounds along with the 7.30am Bradford (Foster Square) to Bristol Temple Meads express, due there around 1.25pm. This was a typical working which did not greatly change over the years, albeit a little slower than in 1938 when it left Bradford at 7.45am, but still arriving in Temple Meads at 1.25pm.   *Michael Mensing*

Above: **Wickwar, May 1935.** A distinguished visitor, 5552 *Silver Jubilee*, is on a down train which has just passed through Wickwar tunnel. 5552, which started life as 5642, undertook a publicity tour of the LMS system in 1935 to commemorate the Silver Jubilee of King George V. The loco was painted in unlined high gloss black and various fittings were chrome-plated. *Real Photographs*

Below: **Wickwar.** More mundane services are represented in the tunnel cutting by 4F 44076 on an express freight. The tunnel was 1401 yards in length according to BR, but 1397 yards in Midland Railway literature! It had a portal at the northern end only; at the southern end the rock was stable enough not to require one. *R K Blencowe collection*

Above: **Yate.** Midland Railway 4-4-0 525 pauses at the station on a rather wet day by the look of it, with a reasonable number of passengers scurrying along the platform. Branch trains to Thornbury, seven and a half miles away, departed from here. Although the passenger service ceased in June 1944, the branch remained open for freight, including Tytherington stone quarries. *Lens of Sutton*

Below: **Yate.** A down express passes through with 'Jubilee' 45725 *Repulse* in charge. Yate Main Line Junction signal box is visible behind the train; the Thornbury branch turned off west at the junction. *R K Blencowe collection*

Above: **Yate South Junction.** The middle two tracks are the main line to and from Mangotsfield; the nearest and furthest lines connect to the GWR Bristol-Swindon route, with the furthest crossing over the Midland lines to gain access to the up side here. 45660 *Rooke* heads the up 'Devonian' which has traversed the GW route out of Temple Meads via Stapleton Road, Stoke Gifford and Westerleigh West Junction rather than the Midland line through Mangotsfield. However the down 'Devonian' – and the Western's 'Cornishman' in both directions – used the Midland line to and from Bristol, as did the majority of Midland passenger trains.   *Real Photographs*

Below: **Stoke Gifford, 1961.** Other Midland workings using the Stoke Gifford route included banana specials. 45598 *Basutoland* approaches Stoke Gifford West signal box with one such train from Avonmouth Docks. The special vans for this traffic were insulated and steam-heated. In the summer 1961 working time table there were four paths for banana trains going from Avonmouth (Old Yard) via Stoke Gifford and Charfield to the LMR, departing at 1pm, 3.15pm, 6.10pm and 10.0pm, all Saturdays excepted. But of course these only ran 'as required'.   *R S Carpenter collection*

Above: **Westerleigh, early 1960s.** 46100 *Royal Scot,* now allocated to 17A Derby, heads the 5pm Bristol to York under GWR bridge 32A, which is on the Bristol and South Wales main line. A rebuilt 'Royal Scot' – 46120 *Royal Inniskilling Fusilier* – appeared on the line in February 1949 with the morning Nottingham-Bristol train; in July 1949 it was working through from York to Bristol on the 12.40pm Newcastle express. But the class did not become regular performers on the route until displaced from other lines by diesels.   *Rex Conway collection*

Below: **Westerleigh sidings, 1964.** At Westerleigh were around a dozen sidings on both the up and down sides of the Midland line. These had been lengthened and added to during the Second World War. It was a major yard, with many Birmingham-Bristol route freights starting, terminating or calling here. There were four signal boxes: North Junction; South Junction; Up Sidings; Down Sidings, but all closed in February 1965, along with the sidings, leaving just the up and down main lines in use. From the beginning of 1970, even that was reduced, to just a single line.Ex-Crosti 2-10-0 92024 hauls a train of vans at the sidings which look busy enough, but it was the last few months for this erstwhile important freight location. Beyer-Garratt locos were working through to here from Toton on a daily basis for a while from 1 March 1950, arriving in the evening and returning next morning on the 6.20am or 7.25am mineral empties.

Above: **Mangotsfield North, 22 April 1957.** About two miles further on was Mangotsfield, where 45509 *The Derbyshire Yeomanry* performs its regular weekday duty, the 7.35am semi-fast Nottingham-Bristol. The train is approaching Mangotsfield North, junction for the line to Bath; this line avoided the station. The Nottingham train was due here at 11.42am and Temple Meads at 11.56am. During the Second World War 'Patriots' worked the very heavy 7.40am from Bristol, usually 15 carriages, and this required three bankers up the Lickey. *R K Blencowe collection*

Below: **Mangotsfield, 5 July 1947.** Compound 1073 of Bournville shed drifts in with the 9.28am Bristol-Gloucester stopper. The Station signal box on the left, situated by the Bath line platform, met an unfortunate fate, being destroyed by fire on 29 January 1967. *H C Casserley*

Mangotsfield station. This had platforms on two sides of the triangle of lines. The first view looking north shows the Gloucester lines on the left, with the Bath lines on the right. The next has been taken from the Gloucester platform looking north; and, overleaf, from the down, Bristol, side with Station signal box in the background.   *Lens of Sutton*

Above: **Mangotsfield, mid-1950s.** 7013 *Bristol Castle* heads for Staple Hill tunnel with a Western Region express. From the summer of 1953 the 'Cornishman' was rerouted between Yate South and Temple Meads via Mangotsfield on Mondays to Friday, while still using the GW route via Stoke Gifford on Saturdays. *R K Blencowe collection*

Staple Hill tunnel and station. 514 yards long, the tunnel was just under a mile from Mangotsfield and opened out into Staple Hill station. Around 17 trains stopped here on weekdays, on Bath and Gloucester services. *D Ibbotson; Stations UK*

Above: **Fishponds.** The station was in business for 100 years, from 1866 to 1966. The first two pictures, looking north and south, appear to be from Midland Railway days. The Avonside Engine Co had a connection here.

R S Carpenter collection; Lens of Sutton

Right: **Fishponds.** An immaculate 45685 *Barfleur* has just surmounted the gradient and is passing through on an up express in the early BR era. Barrow Road 'Jubilees' had a reputation for cleanliness and good mechanical condition. In 1949 the 'Railway Observer' noted: 'Engines from Bristol seem to be more highly polished than ever, a speciality being the gleaming buffers and bright brasswork.'

Real Photographs

FISH PONDS
45685

606
600
L M

BOOKING OFFICE

Left, above: **Clifton Extension Railway.** At Kingswood Junction, less than a mile from Fishponds station, was the connection to the joint GWR/Midland Clifton Extension Railway with stations at Montpelier, Redland and Clifton Down. The CER was linked to the Hotwells and Avonmouth lines, giving access to the important docks at the latter place. Stapleton Road Gas Works, a mile from Kingswood Junction, also connected to the CER and was served by Midland trains.

In LMS days 2P 4-4-0 600 is tender-first at Redland on a Bath Green Park to Clifton Down train, composed of ex-LSWR coaches. Redland was also served by GWR passenger trains between Temple Meads and Avonmouth Docks. 600 later ventured a long way north and spent the whole of its BR existence in Scotland, unlike classmate 601 which was shedded at Bath and, occasionally, Templecombe until withdrawal in 1959.					*Author's collection*

Left, below: **Clifton Down, 1936.** 4F 4134 on the up line does some gentle shunting at Clifton Down. 4134 has a 22A shed plate, being a Barrow Road engine. Before this classification was introduced by the LMS in 1935, Bristol had been shed code 8. Note the poster boards on the platform, both for the GWR and the LMS. Just beyond the station was Clifton Tunnel, 1738 yards long.					*Author's collection*

Above: **Clifton Down, 31 May 1959.** An excellent panorama of the station and yard. According to the 'Handbook of Stations' it could handle: goods traffic; passenger, parcels and miscellaneous traffic; furniture vans, carriages, motor cars, portable engines and machines on wheels; horse boxes and prize cattle vans; carriages and motor cars by passenger or parcels train. The four and a half ton crane was hand operated.   *P J Garland, R S Carpenter collection*

Above: **Lawrence Hill.** Heavy trains out of Bristol usually needed banking assistance, the grade up to Fishponds varying between 1 in 57 and 1 in 69. 44264 is seen pushing vigorously as it passes over the GW main line from Temple Meads to Cardiff. There was a very tall signal by Barrow Road for up trains so that drivers could see if they had the road from a distance and go for it up the bank to Fishponds. A train did not stop for the banker which never coupled on, it just came out behind from the sidings and caught up. *B W L Brooksbank, Initial Photographs*

Below: **Lawrence Hill Junction.** The signal box nestles in the vee of the line to Temple Meads in the foreground and those to St Philips and Avonside Wharf behind it. *R J Essery collection*

Above: **Lawrence Hill station, c.1930.** This was on the GWR's Bristol-Cardiff line, though it did see Bristol-Birmingham trains, such as the up 'Devonian' and other workings such as those which bypassed Temple Meads and went via St Philips Marsh to here, then Stapleton Road and Stoke Gifford to Yate.   *Mowat collection*

The allocation at 22A Bristol in January 1948

2-6-2T 3P	2
4-4-0 2P	1
4-4-0 3P	1
4-4-0 4P	3
0-6-0T 1F	2
0-6-0 3F	11
0-6-0 4F	14
4-6-0 5MT	5
4-6-0 5XP	9
0-4-0T (Sentinel)	1
0-6-0T 3F	3
0-4-0ST 0F	1
0-4-4T 1P	2
0-6-0 2F	1
Total	**56**

Above and previous page, below: **Barrow Road shed, 4 April 1965**. Always worth looking out for – though by the date of this photo and the one on page 71, taken from a passing train, the allocation was somewhat depleted. But it was the last BR steam shed in Bristol, so hosted a real mix of locos in latter days. Class 3 Standard 2-6-2T 82001, seen overleaf, worked on the Bath Green Park service; around a dozen of this class transferred to Barrow Road in August and September 1960. It is standing near the coaling tower, a standard LMS type erected in the late 1930s. The gas holder loomed over the place. *R J Essery collection*

Below: **Barrow Road shed, 16 July 1956**. The interior of the roundhouse is illustrated here. The two ex-Lancashire & Yorkshire saddle tanks were used for shunting Avonside Wharf. When these were withdrawn, others of the class – 51217, 51218 and 51221 – came to Bristol. 51221 was in a collision with a 'Jubilee' at the shed coaling plant in June 1959 in which a driver was injured. Perhaps this contributed to 51221's withdrawal in December 1959. *R M Casserley*

Dr Day's Bridge Junction. Lines to Temple Meads go past the box and the 'Bristol Loop' lines veer off to the left and lead to North Somerset Junction, which is where this freight from the Midlands is seen, hauled by an 8F. It is heading for Bristol East Depot on the Great Western main line to Bath.   *P J Garland / R S Carpenter collection (2)*

LMS RAILWAY
ST PHILIPS
PASSENGER STATION
BOVRIL

Opposite and above: **Bristol St Philips.** This Midland Railway goods and passenger station was a very modest affair. There was a goods depot here by 1858 and it was used for local passenger services from 2 May 1870. The first picture shows an 0-4-4T having arrived on a local from Bath; the second has the single wooden platform. The third sees Bath Green Park's 41240 on three Southern Region coaches at the terminus – which was reported to be in an advanced state of disintegration when the passenger services ceased on 19 September 1953, being transferred to Temple Meads. St Philips became goods only and 41240 was transferred to Barrow Road shed.

Stations UK (1); Author's collection (2)

Above: **Bristol Temple Meads, 1935.** The contrast between Temple Meads and St Philips could not be greater. This view of the frontage and entrance hall of the joint station includes decorations in place to celebrate 'GWR 1835 One Hundred Years of Public Service 1935'. The station was designed for the Midland, Bristol & Exeter and Great Western Railways, with each having an archway to their respective booking offices.

R S Carpenter collection

Right: This publicity postcard of the sights of the city emphasises the joint nature of the railway in Bristol, with travel by both GWR and LMS being encouraged.

Dalkeith Publishing Company

Above and overleaf: **Bristol Temple Meads.** Four views showing various aspects of the station: with platform 12 on the left the first looks into the interior of the 'Midland' side, which was used by trains until September 1965; two views of the joint station train shed as it was prior to the 1930s remodelling – the narrow platforms are particularly noticeable, one of them was squeezed in after removal of the broad gauge in the 1890s; the last dates from 1959 and sees part of Temple Meads after the extensive 1930s reconstruction.   *Stations UK (3); Brunel University, Clinker views*

Above: **Bristol Temple Meads.** Midland Railway Class 2 0-6-0 1930 stands at Temple Meads sometime before 1904, probably on an engineering train. A member of the 1798 Class, it was built in 1890; rebuilt in 1904; renumbered 3257 in 1907; rebuilt again as a Class 3 in 1925; and at the start of BR in 1948 was still around, shedded at Gloucester Barnwood, becoming 43257. *Author's collection*

Below: **Bristol Temple Meads.** 4-4-0 473 in Midland Railway livery presents a fine sight in the Brunel terminus. The loco was originally 2581, built by Beyer Peacock in 1900 to a Johnson design, with 6' 6" driving wheels, but was rebuilt by Deeley in 1905, as seen here, and received the number 473 in the 1907 renumbering scheme. It was withdrawn in June 1927. *Author's collection*

Above: **Bristol Temple Meads.** Compound 4-4-0 1000 arrives at platform 2 on a down express. As already mentioned, Compounds did not work regularly on the line until the LMS era, in the mid-1920s. 1000 had a spell at Gloucester Barnwood shed in the 1930s.
Stations UK

Below: **Bristol Temple Meads, 1935.** Bigger motive power is in the offing as 'Jubilee' 4-6-0 5552 *Silver Jubilee* attracts admirers. This is probably during the publicity tour of the LMS system already mentioned. 'Jubilees' became the top express motive power on LMS trains from Bristol to Birmingham and further north, with Barrow Road having a number – around nine or ten in their heyday – allocated right through to 1964. They were highly regarded and, as already stated, often kept in very clean condition during the 1950s.
R S Carpenter collection

Above: **Bristol Temple Meads, Saturday 6 August 1960.** Barrow Road's own 'Patriot' 45506 *The Royal Pioneer Corps* blows off as it waits to depart with train M232, Paignton to Leeds. The station clock shows the time, 11.50am. The 4F is 44560 a Templecombe-based engine. *B W L Brooksbank / Initial Photographs*

Below: **Bristol Temple Meads, 25 February 1958.** Thoughts of summer Saturday trains seem a distant memory in this icy shot of 44209 with empty stock from the very late running previous night's 7.10pm ex Newcastle. Due in Temple Meads at 5.20am, it actually arrived at 2.55pm after snow in the north disrupted overnight and morning services. *Michael Mensing*

Above: **Bristol Temple Meads.** As dieselisation progressed, 'Jubilees' were transferred *en masse* to sheds such as 21A Saltley, whose 45647 *Sturdee* – formerly an LMR Western Division engine – awaits departure from platform 12 with an overnight parcels. Two regular – and heavily loaded – parcels trains on the route were P482 (later 3N10) 8.15pm to Leeds and P486 (3M25) 11.45pm to Derby. In the Christmas period there were many extra parcels workings – for example one on 17 December 1964 being 3X08 3.10pm Bristol-Newcastle loaded to 15 vans, with another two, from South Wales, being added at Gloucester. *South Devon Railway Museum*

Right, above: **Bristol Temple Meads.** 'The Devonian' was one of two named regular Midland expresses on the Birmingham-Bristol and Bath line – the other being 'The Pines Express'. On 6 August 1956 'The Devonian' changed engines as usual at Temple Meads with the Midland motive power making way for 5024 *Carew Castle* which took the train further west. From the late 1920s, the change was made on occasion at Gloucester. This seems to have happened when the train bypassed Temple Meads on its way through Bristol. In the Summer 1938 working timetable, the equivalent train, 10am Bradford-Paignton, had a GWR reporting number from Gloucester on Saturdays, suggesting the motive power change took place there; Saturday being the only day when the train avoided Temple Meads. *Michael Mensing*

Right, below: **Bristol Temple Meads, 6 August 1956.** Midland and LMS engines worked beyond Bristol to Weston-Super-Mare, 19 miles, and here is unnamed 'Patriot' 45508 arriving from Weston on M856 relief to Sheffield on a Bank Holiday Monday. The loco bears a 10B, Preston, shed plate, making it a pretty rare sighting at Bristol – and an even rarer one at Weston with 'Trains Illustrated' magazine suggesting the appearance of a 'Patriot' at the seaside resort was 'unprecedented'. It had worked into the area on the 7.30am from Bradford two days earlier.

A 1959 working time table list of LMR engines which 'may be employed for through working from Bristol T M to Weston-Super-Mare' included Class 4 freight 0-6-0s as well as various 2-6-0, 4-4-0 and 4-6-0 Classes. *Michael Mensing*

Yatton. A well-loaded excursion with an interesting selection of carriages is seen near Yatton, about 12 miles from Bristol, in the years before the First World War and is probably bound for Weston-Super-Mare. The loco is class 2 0-6-0 3536 of Bournville shed, suggesting the train started at Birmingham. 3536, built in 1897 when it was numbered 2350, remained as a class 2 throughout its long life, becoming BR 58283, and was not withdrawn until March 1961.   *LGRP*

Above: **Mangotsfield, 20 May 1958.** Stanier 0-4-4T had a sojourn on Bristol-Bath locals from 1946, with four – out of the class of 10 – allocated to Green Park. But they gave way in autumn 1949 to brand-new Ivatt Class 2 2-6-2T – 41240/41/42/43. Barrow Road shed also supplied locos for the service and one of their Ivatts, 41207, approaches Mangotsfield. In the last years of steam on the workings, BR Standard Class 3 tanks were regulars.

R S Carpenter collection

Below: **Warmley station.** This was only around a mile and a quarter from Mangotsfield, and is seen here on a rather wet day. Note the very tall signal post with co-acting arms, used due to sighting problems caused by the bridge.

Stations UK

Above: **Warmley station.** Seen here is a down express heading towards Bath behind Caprotti Standard 5 73140. There were 13 Bristol-Bath passenger trains each way stopping here on Monday to Saturday in 1950, including through trains over the Somerset & Dorset to and from Bournemouth. It also had a somewhat skeletal Sunday service.
Author's collection

Below: **Oldland Common.** Just a modest halt, but with the same level of service as Warmley. It was only opened in December 1935.
Lens of Sutton

Bitton. Well-known nowadays as the headquarters of the Avon Valley Railway, but the two pictures here pre-date the preservation era. A Midland 2-4-0 bowls into the station, with a decent number of passengers waiting to board. The other picture is bereft of train, passengers and foliage, but gives a better view of the station buildings, goods shed and signal box. Both views are looking towards Mangotsfield.

There were two bridges over the river Avon from Bitton to the next station, Kelston (closed on and from 1 January 1949), and two more from there to Weston. *Lens of Sutton; Stations UK*

Above: **Weston station.** This was just less than a mile from Bath Green Park. Opened in 1869, when the route from Mangotsfield to Bath came into operation, it was renamed Weston (Bath) station from 1 October 1934. But it did not survive to the end in March 1966, closing to passengers on 19 September 1953. *Lens of Sutton*

Below: **Bath, 25 April 1950.** Some fine Midland Railway wooden signals guard the exit from Bath. Over near the shed is a Midland 3P, apparently in steam, very rare by the date of this photograph. It is probably Templecombe's 40741, the last 3P in the area, withdrawn from Barrow Road in September 1951. *H C Casserley*

Right: **Bath, 23 August 1958.**
The Midland wooden signals have gone in this picture, replaced in June 1956. But the old Midland shed of two roads still houses working 4-4-0s, as well as an unrebuilt 'West Country' Pacific visible behind 41249. In the background is Bath Green Park station.   *P Chancellor collection*

Below: **Bath station.**
Two local trains at Bath with typical motive power for the Midland Railway era – a 2-4-0 and 0-4-4T, both with Salter safety valves and round top firebox.
     Lens of Sutton; H C Casserley

Above: **Bath Green Park, August 1950.** Another type used on Bristol-Bath stoppers was the Stanier 2-6-2T, represented by Barrow Road's 40174. A double-headed train for the Somerset & Dorset line waits for the road before starting the ascent out of Bath. Bath Station signal box is in the background, with the Midland loco shed on the right.

H F Wheeller, R S Carpenter collection

Below: **Bath Green Park.** Templecombe shed's 4F 44417 stands at Green Park while the driver converses with station staff and a rake of Southern coaches await their next duty.　　　　*Late Rev John Parker, Hugh Davies collection*

Above: **Bath Green Park, 15 September 1951.** Arriving off the Somerset & Dorset line are 2P 40564 and 'West Country' 34044 *Woolacombe*. This train is no doubt bound for points north, via Mangotsfield, Gloucester and Birmingham, after a change of motive power. 34044 was one of five 'West Country' Pacifics – 34040 to 34044 – allocated to Bath shed at the time.

R M Casserley

The allocation at 22C Bath in January 1948	
2-6-2T 3P	1
4-4-0 2P	8
4-4-0 4P	1
0-4-4T 2P	4
0-6-0 4F	11
4-6-0 5MT	5
0-4-0T (Sentinel)	1
0-6-0T 3F	6
0-4-0ST 0F	1
2-8-0 7F	11
0-4-4T 1P	1
Total	**50**

Overleaf: **Bath loco shed.** The Somerset & Dorset Railway loco depot at Bath was larger than the Midland's – though by the date of these photos, the two had been merged into one. An S&D 2P 4-4-0, No.15, with round top firebox, reposes on shed on 24 May 1929. 15 was designed by Johnson and built at Derby in 1891, though somewhat rebuilt here from its original condition. On 1 January 1930, the LMS took over all S&D locos and 15 became LMS 301. But not for long, as it was withdrawn in 1931. S&D loco 13806, a large-boilered 2-8-0, stands in the shed yard in 1935. These engines did escape the S&D from time to time and find their way northwards onto the Bristol- Birmingham line – and not only when they went to Derby Works for overhaul. A particularly interesting sighting at Gloucester, where they were seen quite regularly, was one double-heading the up 'Pines Express' in the early 1950s.

H C Casserley; Rex Conway collection

Above: **Bath, 12 August 1961.** BR's most modern power was represented on the S&D, with several 9Fs shedded at Bath. One of them, 92006 starts its journey from Bath with the train 1O94, the 7.43am Bradford-Bournemouth; this arrived at Bath behind 45690 *Leander*. It was but one of the long-distance trains this summer Saturday which had travelled down from the north via Birmingham and Mangotsfield. Other arrivals included 1O88 with 73087 *Linette*; 1O91 with 44918; 1O93 with 44857; 1O95 with 92136; 1O97 with 73155. But the following summer was to be the last to see such frantic activity at Bath, with these summer trains, and the 'Pines Express' itself, being diverted to other routes from the start of the winter timetable in September 1962.   *A C Gilbert*

Below: **Bath loco depot, 1966.** A bird's-eye view of the loco depot in its dying days, the S & D shed is in the foreground, the coal stage to the right and the Midland shed behind with out-of-use locos alongside it. Green Park station is in the background.   *R K Blencowe collection*

Bath, Somerset & Dorset line, August 1956. It would not be right to leave without seeing a train on S&D tracks proper, so here is a Bournemouth bound express behind 40563 and 73050 on the single line, with Bath as a backdrop. The S&D diverged from the Mangotsfield line at Bath Junction, half a mile out of Green Park station, and trains were then faced with a stiff climb out of the city on a ruling gradient of 1 in 50 for nearly four miles to Midford.
Norman Simmons, Hugh Davies collection

Inset: Both the GWR and LMS were keen to promote 'Historic Bath' as a destination for potential passengers.

Dalkeith Publishing Company

Incidents and Accidents

21 October 1935, Churchdown. Driver A G Nipper was reprimanded for failing to stop as booked on the 8.20pm Worcester – Bristol passenger.

26 May 1936, Gloucester. Passed Fireman F J Cains got severely reprimanded for overrunning the home signal while working the 10.35am passenger from Bristol.

20 March 1940, Tuffley Junction. Driver F Barnett was suspended for one day after passing signals at danger on the 11.10am Leeds-Bristol.

21 September 1960, Haresfield. Standard '5MT' 73136 had a serious failure while working the 7.0pm class 'D' Bristol to Derby. The right hand connecting rod became detached from the crosshead. Damage done to the loco – 'Right connecting rod badly bent and split. Right cylinder cover broken. Right piston rod bent. Right gudgeon pin broken. Right front coupling rod bent and gradient pin damaged.' It was six hours before the train got under way again, with 4F 43911.

22 December 1937, Stonehouse. Driver J H Davies was reprimanded for failing to stop at Stonehouse as booked on the 12 noon Bradford-Bristol express, with engine 5609.

10 April 1947, Stonehouse and Frocester. Driver H F G Huntley received a commendation for promptly calling attention to defective permanent way between the two places.

4 November 1932, Coaley Junction. Driver F G Kerton was suspended for one day after passing a home signal at danger, thereby causing a mishap. Engine was 3461.

October 9 1963, Coaley. Barnwood's 73068 suffered a mechanical defect while working the 10.5pm stopping passenger from Bristol to Gloucester, 2H74. On running into the station, the right hand side eccentric rod broke causing engine failure. The train was delayed 101 minutes, a fresh engine coming from Gloucester.

17 June 1936, Wickwar. Fireman L Harrison was severely reprimanded for allowing a fire iron to fall off his engine 5097 on the 4.43pm Derby-Bristol passenger, which came into contact with engine 521 working an up passenger train.

9 September 1934, Charfield. Passed Fireman E J S Hardy was severely reprimanded for failing to stop on excursion train 408, Bristol to Birmingham, with engine 748.

30 June 1902, Yate. Fireman Asher Benjamin Ackerman was reprimanded for leaving the train's guard behind.

26 July 1904, Thornbury. Passed cleaner A I Jacques was fined 3/6d for want of care in moving an engine and causing damage to the shed doors.

5 February 1926, Westerleigh sidings. Driver R I Boulton was severely reprimanded for passing a signal at danger, running through points and damaging them.

2 March 1926, Westerleigh. Passed Fireman J Stevens was reprimanded for failing to travel on the 1.0am light engine from Barrow Road to Westerleigh, thereby necessitating the running of a special light engine for him and his fireman.

11 September 1948, Westerleigh sidings. Fireman S K Wait was awarded two guineas for assisting Shunter R H Golledge to calve a cow which was in transit from Lanark to Umberleigh.

4 August 1922, Mangotsfield. Passed Fireman H J Evans got reprimanded for giving improper whistles here and not whistling at Warmley, causing delay to his train.

12 August 1924, Mangotsfield. Fireman A Graves had a reprimand put on his record after 'having boiler of engine too full resulting in damage to glass in roof at the station, owing to safety valve blowing off.'

I June 1933, Coalpit Heath. Driver G W Thomas was cautioned for allowing his engine, 3595, to overrun, damaging a crossing gate.

6 April 1892, Fishponds. Fireman Samuel Ludwell was suspended for one week for 'neglect of duty, causing collision with a passenger train.'

14 September 1930, Staple Hill. Passed Fireman A E Garrard was severely reprimanded for failing to stop as booked with a special passenger train, hauled by loco 4534.

15 May 1941, Barrow Road. A passed fireman had a reprimand for allowing engine 1035 to emit volumes of black smoke over Barrow Road bridge and, at the same time, committing a personal nuisance under it!

6 January 1943, Barrow Road. Driver E G Hill was cautioned after engine 5432 was overcoaled at the coaling plant.

1 March 1947, Barrow Road. Drivers F J Griffiths and A Simons were cautioned after contributing to a collision in the loco yard between engines 2769 and 4829, which caused a delay of 11 minutes to the 10.30am passenger.

11 December 1941, Lawrence Hill. Driver F J Fellows passed the main home and starting signals at danger, with Southern Railway 388 (class K10 4-4-0), for which misdemeanour he got a severe reprimand.

19 August 1959, Lawrence Hill. Driver S Cooper received a strong verbal caution – loco 44411 was derailed after semaphore signal 42 was passed at danger.

26 May 1950, Bristol St Philips. Driver C Thomas got a caution after engine 44569 was derailed in the carriage sidings. (This was the fifth derailment noted against Driver Thomas!)

19 September 1953, Temple Meads. Driver H H Crosse was cautioned for passing signals 149 and 151 at danger and running through point 141.

30 November 1933, Stapleton Road Gas Works. Driver H F G Huntley and Passed Fireman F E Barnes were cautioned for failing to carry out rule 142(d), which, briefly, states that the driver should ensure at the start of a journey that the fireman and guard have exchanged signals to confirm that the guard is in his van and the train is complete. Their loco was class 2 0-6-0 3062.

13 September 1926, Clifton Down. Driver A G Nipper was reprimanded for engine 3593 being low in steam, causing delay to a train.

15 November 1937, Avonmouth. Driver F Bryant was reprimanded for passing a ground disc at danger, causing engine 3186 to be derailed.

18 December 1934, Kelston. Driver L Board was cautioned for failing to observe a speed restriction at bridge no. 28.

22 September 1953, Oldland Common. Driver E Exton failed to stop with the 6.5am passenger, earning himself a caution.

17 December 1932, Bath. Passed Fireman W J V Bryant was cautioned after loco 3461 derailed in the yard due to his not holding the points properly.

4 August 1935, Bath. Driver J M Harnett had a one day suspension after his engine 4135 derailed on the shed turntable, causing damage. On 20 February 1936, he was reprimanded after a similar incident here with engine 2729.

Details have been taken mainly from personnel records and loco casualty reports. Dates in bold are the actual dates of the incidents shown. Other dates are those entered on the personnel records – the incidents could have occurred anytime from same date to several weeks previously. Most of the crews mentioned were based at Bristol Barrow Road shed. No doubt men from other loco depots which worked the line over the years had similar misadventures!

Further Selected Bibliography

An Historical Survey of the Midland in Gloucestershire *Peter Smith*

Bristol & Gloucester Railway *Colin Maggs*

Mangotsfield to Bath Branch *Colin Maggs*

Lines to Avonmouth *Mike Vincent*

Track Layout Diagrams Bristol; South Gloucestershire *R A Cooke*

Articles on Bristol: August 1909; September, October and November 1956 *Railway Magazine*

Midland Railway Society journals

British Locomotive Catalogue 1825-1923, Vol. 3A – Midland Railway *Bertram Baxter*

'The Talk of the Line – Barrow Road's Jubilees' – January 1996 *Steam World magazine*

'Station Survey Temple Meads' – June-July 1992 *British Railways Illustrated magazine*

While every effort has been made to obtain permission from owners of copyright materials reproduced herein, the publisher would like to apologise for any omissions and will be pleased to incorporate missing acknowledgements in any future editions.

And finally...

Defford, 14 May 1960. Being a long-distance cross-country route meant unfamiliar engines could appear at any time, having been 'borrowed' from their usual turns. You never knew what might turn up, but the photographer was fortunate to be at the lineside when ex-LNER K3 2-6-0 61853 assisted old favourite 45662 *Kempenfelt* with the 12.48pm York-Bristol. This was not a unique appearance by a K3, although the class always remained very rare on the line. The working time table specifically mentioned the type, saying 'The engines are permitted to work between Barnt Green and Bristol via Dunhampstead subject to the observance of all speed restrictions applicable to engines in the 'RED' group.'

Tim Farebrother